"The Gospel According to a Modern Day Sinner"

TO: DAVE MORGAN

Dave, Dispite our miscommunication no matter where the fault. I want you to know I have enjoyed many of our conversations. I TOLD YOU I WOULD GIVE YOU a copy of my book when I am done so here it is. MAY God Bless you & GOD's Speed.

ITHESS
1:5

© Copyright 2005 Gregg C. Cummings.
All rights reserved. No part of this publication may be reproduced, stored in a retrieval system, or transmitted, in any form or by any means, electronic, mechanical, photocopying, recording, or otherwise, without the written prior permission of the author.

Note for Librarians: a cataloguing record for this book that includes Dewey Decimal Classification and US Library of Congress numbers is available from the Library and Archives of Canada. The complete cataloguing record can be obtained from their online database at: www.collectionscanada.ca/amicus/index-e.html
ISBN 1-4120-5839-2
Printed in Victoria, BC, Canada

Printed on paper with minimum 30% recycled fibre.
Trafford's print shop runs on "green energy" from solar, wind and other environmentally-friendly power sources.

TRAFFORD

Offices in Canada, USA, Ireland and UK

This book was published *on-demand* in cooperation with Trafford Publishing. On-demand publishing is a unique process and service of making a book available for retail sale to the public taking advantage of on-demand manufacturing and Internet marketing. On-demand publishing includes promotions, retail sales, manufacturing, order fulfilment, accounting and collecting royalties on behalf of the author.

Book sales for North America and international:
Trafford Publishing, 6E–2333 Government St.,
Victoria, BC V8T 4P4 CANADA
phone 250 383 6864 (toll-free 1 888 232 4444)
fax 250 383 6804; email to orders@trafford.com
Book sales in Europe:
Trafford Publishing (UK) Ltd., Enterprise House, Wistaston Road Business Centre,
Wistaston Road, Crewe, Cheshire CW2 7RP UNITED KINGDOM
phone 01270 251 396 (local rate 0845 230 9601)
facsimile 01270 254 983; orders.uk@trafford.com
Order online at:
trafford.com/05-0739

10 9 8 7 6 5 4 3 2

Dedication

I want to dedicate this book to my two beautiful daughters Tasha Alexandria and Alora Lyzette. Together watching you two grow up has kept my heart light in my times of grief and sorrow. I know that at times I have made life miserable for you but I know too that I have made some times happy for you as well. Throughout my life I have made many bad decisions and have not been the role model for you that I would like, in fact it wasn't till late that I am finally getting a grasp of what the Lord has for us all to know. And it is this knowledge I have written about in this book.

These pages are dedicated to you both, Tasha and Alora. I hope and pray that you read this message and take heed to the knowledge you'll find and begin your quest in your own lives now without waiting until you're my age. God has a plan for you both and only He knows that plan and it is there for you to seek out. You both have made me very proud and I know if you choose to follow God in all things that He will use your talents greatly.

Go with my love and my support, May God Bless you both,
 as always;
~Your Dad

Introduction

When I was very young I never thought that I would ever read a whole book, let alone write one. Then to write one about the Gospel is an even greater surprise. My whole life has been a roller coaster of trials, most of which I seemed to have failed. As I look back I realize God has never left me, but, believe me when I say, I sure do not know why other than His enormous grace He has for all of us. I never really grew up in a church going family. We all believed in God but never considered ourselves real Christians.

One day when I was thirty-eight, a friend said I should write a book. I then received motivation about a month later to write one, not any book, but this book. I felt I needed to title it "The Gospel According to Gregg," but very quickly realized I should not equate myself to the apostles by any means, for I know I am not worthy of that stature. So, almost as quick as I thought to name it the above title, I was enlightened with the following words; "You are a sinner, so name it as such." So that is where the title came from. The Gospel According To A Modern Day

Sinner.

The word gospel means "good news" and is used for terms of truth and of the life and teachings of our Lord Jesus Christ. I was moved to write about this because we live in a time when we are vastly becoming immune to the Gospel, or, maybe better put, we are becoming desensitized to constantly hearing the Word while indulging in the worldly "feel good" things that are bombarding us on a daily basis. The apostles also lived in a time when they too had their work cut out for them, and the Mathew, Mark, Luke, and John's writings became the very gospels we are speaking of now, as well as David, and maybe as a side not for these gospels, some 2000 years later, this book might help some of you who are in my same situation: believers who are sinners stuck in a world so evil that no society has ever seen it this bad before; believers who are sinners that want nothing more but the strength and power to break away from the very things that are holding us bound to this way of life; believers who are sinners that feel like losers who cannot give up those "feel good" things that have a more physical reality; sinners that are believers through hope and wanting to be on the right side, and yet not wanting to give up luxuries until we really have to, the "just in case" mentality, the selfish self, that is not always in agreeance with our minds' moral standing.

I only hope you read this book with an open mind to God. If He shows you that what you read is no good, then so be it, for I am not God. I only know that I am a Sinner that is a Believer that wants to share with you from my understanding of the scriptures and not from my selfish desires. Because I believe that God has been with me, I believe that He has taught me understandings that must be preached and must be written down. If this book does nothing else but allow you to know that you are precious in His sight and that He wants you to come to Him with all your being, then I will be happy.

I pray this prayer for you; Oh God my eternal Father, how great are Your ways. I pray for those who read this book that, if I am not writing understandings that You Yourself have given me, then please Oh Lord, do not allow me to deceive them, for I only want to do Thy Will, Oh God, and if this be Your Will, may a blessing fall upon those who read, so they too can find your rod of iron and hold fast, so that they may have the courage and strength to accomplish their calling for Thy Glory, and Thy Kingdom. AMEN.

Table of Contents

Dedication

Introduction

Table of Contents

Chapter One, A Life Spiritual Testimony of the Author   10

Chapter Two, Communion Awareness   34

Chapter Three, The Four Garden Tools   52

Chapter Four, Living The Church   84

Chapter Five, Finding Your Way   101

Chapter Six, The Kingdom of God vs.
the Great Abominable Church   122

Chapter Seven, Making a Covenant   151

Chapter Eight, The Gospel Purpose   173

Chapter Nine, Some Final Thoughts   191

"And unto man he said, Behold, the fear of the Lord, that is wisdom; and to depart from evil is understanding."

~Job 28:28, K.J.V.

Chapter One
A Life Spiritual Testimony of the Author

I am going to write this in the best way I know how. My hope is only that I write in an understandable way, but there are no guarantees. I am going to tell this from my perspective, for there are others in my life that share the same memories, but like anyone all might have different takes on the happenings so take it for what it is worth.

I was born in an average income military family. By then my father was fifty-one years old and a WWII, Korean and Vietnam War veteran and closing in on his retirement from the armed forces. My mother was twenty-three years old and a good mom. I was the youngest, along with my twin brother, Grant. I had two older brothers as well, Grover and Grady. My twin and I were five years old when my father finally retired, and this is where my memories really begin.

It is important for you and me that I explain how my family was in my eyes to help you understand some things later.

My father was born in 1914 and grew up a very rough individual. Being on his own since the age of thirteen, my father had to survive the best way he could. Prior to his military career he boxed small time fights, ran moonshine, and worked as a body guard, a gangster in the truest sense of the term. He eventually owned his own bar in Dayton, Ohio, and frequently hosted other gangsters overnight during their trips between Chicago and New York. Dad even knew John Dillinger and would laugh about what a terrible poker player he was. Even though my father was not a good role model at this point in his life, but by the time we were born, later on in his life, there were some great qualities he had that he taught us boys as we were growing up. These were to not lie, cheat, or steal and that a man's word is his bond and that we should have patriotism for our country. Because of this he became my first teacher in life. While my mom and dad were still married, I thought I was living the American dream. My mom was a very traditional mom and was always there to care for us, and my dad was the strong provider who disciplined us when we were bad. Then, when I was in fifth grade, my parents divorced. My dad was retired, and we were living in Arlington, a small town in Nebraska. This is where, for all of us, I'm sure, our American dream shattered. This is where my testimony begins.

I found out that my mom and dad were divorcing when my mother and three brothers called me into the dining room to tell me. I couldn't understand how they all had stories of so many bad things my dad had done to my mom, and I didn't see this. This was when my oldest brother was labeled a hippie by my dad, a kid that drank, did drugs and played in a rock and roll band. As a matter of fact, it didn't even seem like a couple of weeks after my dad left before our living room became a practice room for his band. At the time, my next oldest brother seemed to be always mean and greedy to me and Grant. He seemed to be a loner and to hang out with our oldest brother. My twin brother became my mom's best friend and protector when she was sad or argued with his brothers. Don't get me wrong, I'm not saying that my brothers are bad people but we all have our faults, as did I. Back then, I just wanted to escape everything and go into my own world most of the time. I had a bad stuttering problem, and everyone, including my brothers, would make fun of me. I felt though that my twin brother could understand how I felt when I was teased because once and awhile he would stick up for me.

    Because of my stuttering and being ridiculed by everyone from such a young age, I began fighting a lot at school and around town. I pretended to my brothers that it never bothered me. Slowly but surely I began lying about it, and soon after that about a lot of things. So, through the teasing and badgering, I slowly became a lying, cheating kid who went totally against that which my father, who was no longer around, had tried to instill. Soon after that, selfishness was added to the new me.

    Then one morning during the summer, the local swimming pool was to open for the summer and my brothers and I couldn't wait to be first in line. When we got up that morning we all dressed in our bathing suits, got our towels and waited for the time to leave. We were all excited and couldn't wait. When it was finally time to leave, all four of us were heading out the door when, the only way I can explain it, a huge presence engulfed me. It was a feeling of pausing, yet calming peace. Then a voice spoke to me in a way that I heard loud and clear, as is if you said something to me, except it seemed to come from within me. It told me to sit down and wait. Not knowing why, and without questions at first, I sat down. My twin brother yelled at me to come on and all I said was to go ahead and I would catch up in a minute. Just minutes before this my mother had told us all to be careful and that she was going to take a shower. You see, my mom is totally deaf in one ear and wears a hearing aid in the other. So, when she takes the hearing aid out, she becomes almost 95% deaf. Anyway, I really wanted to go swimming, and I started to get up when the voice again told me to sit down and wait. This time, after I sat back down, I asked the voice, "Why?" Then I heard an explosion and a huge cloud of smoke and black suet came bellowing over my head. I turned and looked into the kitchen, where the bathroom door was and I saw the whole back wall on fire from the stove. My mother was taking a shower and did not hear a thing. I banged and banged on the door until it opened, and I ran in yelling to my mom who was in the shower that the house was on fire. We both got out safely. My family spent the next few weeks in a motel until the damage was fixed. To this day, I know that the voice was God or an angel of God.

About a month later, I remember walking along my Sunday paper route, and, as I had done a hundred times before, I walked past a certain family's house on my way back home. At that point, a very different feeling surrounded me. I didn't hear a sound or see anything that caught my eye, but I was just overwhelmed by fear. Then suddenly my head twisted uncontrollably to my right and I found myself staring into the family's garage. It was deep space black. All I knew was that there was a presence of something very bad, so I dropped my papers and ran home as fast as I could. I slammed into my mom's bedroom and kept shouting, "There's something bad that the "families name" house!" over and over. When my mom finally calmed me down, she called the family. When the mother of the family checked the garage she found their son dead of a suicide, and a note saying how he was sorry for raping his girlfriend. To this day I know that the feeling I experienced was the presence of pure evil, or the devil.

 These two first hand spiritual experiences came in the same summer when I was eleven years old and were from two totally different sources.

 These were the extent of the encounters with what I call spiritual presence until many years later. All the way to the eighth grade my home life seemed to just get worse. My mom was looking for someone to love her as she needed to be loved and appreciated, but she looked in all the wrong places. Meanwhile my older brothers continued their quest for sex, drugs, and rock-n-roll. I remember, my twin and I were eventually taken to nightclubs and bars to watch my oldest brother play in his bands, this was at a time when children could go into bars with parents so you could guess what kind of role models we had. At this time, a man promised my mom the world, and we moved to Iowa. It wasn't long after that, that I wrote my father at the Old Soldiers' Home in Washington, D.C. to come and get me. He did, and we moved to Pascagoula, Mississippi, where I continued to fight due to my stuttering, except this time my dad got me to go to a boxing club to learn how to fight. During this time, good and evil again were evident in my life. The good was that I was in Jr. High School, and I was led to start wondering more about God and who He was, and who out there knew which "church" was the right church. My father was a Roman Catholic and taught me what was right and wrong in the world's terms, but couldn't help me in any religious matters other than he believed in God. Then it seemed that at the same time I began to wonder about God, the adversary (devil) began to relate to me through my worldly connections from my background and upbringing. I started experimenting with drinking and drugs myself because of my character and the peer groups I associated with. Soon, believe it or not, I was going to all kinds of different denominations on my own every Sunday, and drinking and doing drugs on the Fridays and Saturdays before. I was fourteen years old.

Then a man, Elbert Jackson, started talking with me. He lived in the same condominium as I did. He used to be a running back for the Kansas City Chiefs before a car wreck that tore up his knee, and then he worked as a counselor at the school I went to. Shortly after the good Lord brought him to me, and he mentored me for a while on his own accord, I started to slow down my bad habits. Then I felt God was leading me to go back to Iowa to be with my mom and twin brother, so I wrote them and they came down and got me and took me back as my next older brother Grady stayed and took my place there in Mississippi. I was not expecting what I found, that is for sure.

I moved back with my mom where I discovered my oldest

17

brother Grover had been kicked out or left home at 17 yrs of age and was living by himself in the neighboring town of Lamoni, Iowa, so that just left my twin brother, mom, her alcoholic husband and myself. Even though I went to school in Mt. Ayer, Iowa, we were in Lamoni most of the time. That is when the Lord led me to see this beautiful girl who I knew at that very moment, I mean at that very instant, that I would defiantly marry her in the future. That messenger was with me and let me know that this was true. After we met, we wanted to date, so she introduced me to her father. It wasn't long after that that I knew he was my next teacher in life. I found myself going to my first church youth camp and continuing my search for the right church. After being back with my mom and twin for just a little while, I woke up one night to a lot of screaming. I looked at my twin brother's bed and found it was empty. I threw on a pair of jeans and went to see what the commotion was all about. That is when I saw my brother shielding my mom from her husband, who had just smashed a coffee cup over my mom's face. She was crying hysterically and had cuts all over her face with blood streaming all over the place. My mom's husband was yelling at both of them to get out of the house and I could tell how drunk he was. I looked on in shock. I then noticed he had his handgun lying on the table beside him. He threatened to shoot them if they didn't leave. He was so drunk he forgot that I had returned from Mississippi. When he noticed me, he said, "You too, you little @#%. Get out!" I told him, "No" and he then came after me. About twenty-five minutes later I had him all bloody and passed out on my brother's bed. We packed up what we could and moved to Lamoni that night. I was fifteen years old.

The next day my twin brother and I went back to get the rest of our things. My mom's husband wasn't around, so it made things a lot easier. I remember walking around the farm pondering what was going on in my life. That is when I took a sling that I had made at church camp, (while studying about David and Goliath), and began slinging rocks at the side of the barn, yelling challenges at the top of my lungs to satan. I was daring him to show himself. I would take him down like David did Goliath. Of course nothing happened, but, at the time, it sure made me feel better.

The following year I started school in Lamoni Iowa and

continued seeing the girl who, for the first time since I was a young child, made me feel special; and, to add to that, she gave me the compassion I was so much in need of. By this time most of my youth involved cussing, lying, fighting, drinking and drugs; and I definitely looked the part with my poor clothes, long hair, and the peers I hung out with. So, even though God had placed before me fantastic blessings with my girlfriend and her family, I still kept doing some of those bad habits behind their backs. It was all I knew. I found myself living in two different worlds, one good with my girlfriend and her family, and one bad with my own family atmosphere and the peers I was used to. Believe me this is not an attempt to justify my wrong doings only an explanation of my situation.

The next summer I was baptized during a two-week church youth caravan. I really wanted this to happen. The love and peace I was learning and experienced were incredible.

I did not want it to end because even then I knew I was not strong enough to make it last. But I had to. It wasn't long before I was on that road, sliding in and out of the same rut. I remember asking God to show me what I needed to do. This time I became more aware of God's presence, and, although less and less, my bad habits still lingered. I knew God was there because, for the first time, I felt the guilt of knowing. Knowing these things were wrong for me spiritually as well as physically. It seemed that the only time I was happy, or felt really at home and safe, was when I was with my girlfriend and her family. Ken Tousley, my girlfriend's father, really introduced me to our Lord Jesus Christ. He showed me that the Word of God exists and is alive, and that His Word is found not just in one book but many through out time. I remember coming into the house seeking my girlfriend and Ken would say Gregg sit down for a minute and let me read you something really short. He would then read from the scriptures stories that sometimes lasted over an hour. Maria, (my girlfriend) would come into the room and just smile at me as I would grin and continue to listen to her father. Ken was so understanding of me, of who I was on the inside. I'll go to my grave thanking God for him. During this period of my life, I really made it hard on Maria. She had to endure my lies and deceitfulness. But God, for some reason, gave her the strength to stick with me.

At eighteen years of age I married my girlfriend, Maria, and that ended my drug habits. I became a father working as a bartender by night, and during the day a factory worker, woodcutter, and restaurant worker, depending on what day it was. I was sick and tired of the high society types who frowned on who I was. I wanted to be respected for once in my life. I couldn't help but think of how my dad's presence commanded respect, and of my visions of how my own family would be towards me. My study in the Word never completely stopped, always being kick started again by Maria and Ken. My growth in prayer and meditation kept increasing and there was a point when I again felt a loose connection to the Holy Ghost. Eventually I was led to follow in my father's footsteps and join the Army. At that time, I remember feeling that maybe, just maybe; I could get some respect from others around me.

I spent twelve long years serving my country in what I believed to be the hardest place to be a Christian. My marriage to Maria struggled from time to time only to be, it seemed, forced back into prayer and study which gave us strength. Again God blessed Maria with the tenacity to put up with the military hardships of an elite soldier who was gone most of the year. She was forced into being a single parent for our two beautiful daughters, Tasha and Alora.

I remember one day when I was in the Mojave Desert in California and an armed personnel carrier had picked my partner and I up after three days of being on our own in a desert training environment. As we were traveling, the Lord spoke to me in the familiar voice that I heard so long ago. It startled me at first because it had been so long but then He said, "Gregg, you're not a killing man. There is something for you to do, just not now." I knew it would be found in Lamoni, Iowa. What it was, I did not know.

God sent me all over the world during my military carrier, Honduras, Nicaragua, Panama, Puerto Rico, Germany, Iraq, Saudi Arabia, Haiti and other places. While stationed in Germany, God worked with me to see American history in a different light, which I wrote down but are not a part of this book. God led me to see different cultures and peoples, as well as seeing and experiencing things which were simply horrific. He gave me experiences for reasons I have yet to understand. Then a series of bad things happened to me after I was again stationed in the States. First my father died of cancer, then I found out my twin brother didn't feel the same way about me as I did about him, which I don't expect very many people to understand. Both of these were devastating to me.

Then I remember a day when I was at the Jump Master School at Ft. Bragg, North Carolina. I needed Maria to bring our extra set of car keys because I had locked mine in my car that I had there on the base. She brought them to me on my break I had during the school I was attending so while she and my youngest daughter were there we decided to get a snack for Alora, who had to come with Maria because she was only three years old. While we started towards the snack truck for some reason Maria stopped and called out to me. She didn't know why she had to look in her purse, but she knew she had to. Also she thought someone called to her from behind. That was all the time needed to save our lives, about 10 seconds. We found ourselves between two large trees when a fireball crashed into the ground just fifteen yards in front of us, right in the path where we were heading. The fireball was an F-16 fighter jet that had caught on fire from a mid-air collision with a C-130 transport plane. It smashed to the ground and instantly I was on my way to seek cover, as I had been trained a thousand times to do. Then I realized that my wife and daughter were there with me. I stopped and turned to see Maria facing towards me with Alora in her arms in front of her, while her back was toward the onslaught of debris. I got them on the ground with Alora on the bottom, then Maria, and then myself on top of them. All I can remember thinking is, "God, please keep us safe." We felt a rush of heat go over us and yet there was nothing hitting us. There was however a lot of carnage going on around us. As we all sat up Maria yelled, "Gregg, all those soldiers are on fire!" I looked at her and asked if she was okay. After I assured that they were both fine, I told her to take Alora and go in the opposite direction as I ran into the chaos and helped everyone I could. The jet had crashed into 300+ soldiers preparing to go on a jump just thirty yards from where we were. There is no doubt that God again interceded in our lives, sparing us for unknown reasons other than to help those poor soldiers. The two large trees we were between had shrapnel from the ground to about twenty-five feet up in their branches, and there were hum-vees sitting right next to them that had burnt and melted from the jet fuel. My oldest daughter, Tasha, was still in school at that time of day. I was twenty eight years old.

Two years later I left military services after I fulfilled my last enlistment, a total of twelve years of services, for a number of reasons: first, I felt a calling to come back to Lamoni to help my father-in-law, Ken Tousley, out of life's situations in the same way he had helped his in-laws. Second, I felt it was time to further my Christian faith because I was not doing so in the army. Third, I wanted my daughters to go to school in Lamoni. Fourth, I wanted to leave my military career with a clean record. Finally, I wanted to save my marriage since the stressors that would have accumulated if I had stayed might have destroyed it, for the condition I had put it in at that point needed God's grace and loving intervention. I believe this attack on my life was from satan because he knew that God had prepared a path for me. The adversary knew my weaknesses which he could manipulate.

By this time I was thirty years old, and God had worked throughout my life opening doors. Of those many doors, though, I opened only a few, and that is a shame. The transition into the civilian sector was not one that was going to be easily done. Over that period of time a barrage of good and evil things came at my family and I. First were the past events which attacked my marriage, but God's insights and forgiveness came as a result of prayer and fasting. Then, my best friend in high school was killed over a drug deal. He had told me two days earlier that he wanted to quit like I had and settle down with his new daughter. Then my nephew, who was in his 20's, decided he wanted to be baptized. Shortly after that was when Ken Tousley, my support, my friend, and my father in-law was diagnosed with cancer. God blessed us with the inspiration, ambition, knowledge, and help to build Ken and my mother-in-law, Cirila, a new home to replace their old one that was over 100 years old and falling apart. This made Ken feel at ease with the assurance that his wife would have a good home to live in. Shortly after they moved in, Ken passed away. These events occurred over a three-year time period.

My wife and I started becoming more active in a church and tried our best to mend broken ties. We both received blessings. The Lord then told me that I should speak my mind to the people of the world, to love them, and to make them feel that they are precious and of great worth in the sight of the Lord; that there is a world of difference from my past years and my years ahead; that He has given me a companion that is marvelous, wonderful and precious in His sight and that she might support me in all that I do. I was thirty-three years old.

There is so much more that I will not get into at this time. Through more prayer and fasting the Lord God called to me and told me to prepare myself for a future calling. This came in that same familiar voice that I am now clearly aware of.

At the same time, God had a series of events happen to guide my future career in a different direction that I had previously thought of. I finished college after leaving the military, and changed my major to Sociology and Human Services. I began mentoring troubles teens, which felt really natural to me. Then I felt God inspiring me to create a youth center, but not just any youth center, one that was to bring together the community to combat youth problems and draw in the truly at-risk children. God had inspired great ideas of programming to be housed in the center. It seems to me to be modeled after the Zionic conditions some are striving to achieve through selflessness and love for our neighbors children. I understand that it was not to be mistaken as a start for Zion, just a positive model and example for our youth. Then, like always, as soon as God gives me a blessing or I try to work good, the adversary is not far behind in trying to sabotage that which I do for others. I soon gave the youth center over to the city of Lamoni and was hired at a new residential facility for at-risk teens at the Decatur County Hospital. I became a family counselor and developed a seven-phase program for the residential unit. The program was again modeled on the foundation of the Bible and it's principles. Then I felt that through trials and tribulations in my own life, I had grown to a point where the adversary was going to have to work harder on my weaknesses. My understanding of the Word and workings of the Holy Ghost in my life were at levels that they had never been before. Then the pastor of our denomination came to me saying the Lord told him about my calling, and that he would find me sitting in my yard, and that he was to tell me. Before this I had not mentioned it to no one except Maria. When he did find me sitting in my yard, he explained that he was told I was to be called into the priesthood and that other callings would come later. This was such a great joy and verification to me because it was just a little while prior to that that I had humbly shared only with my wife that I knew a calling was coming forth soon. I was thirty-four years old.

There were two understandings I was having during this time. One was that the Lord had been letting me be aware of the blessings I had and continue to receive in my life, and the other was my current undeserving condition, and that I must continue to pray, fast and purify my life so that I might come to a fuller understanding of what it is that God was communication to me. Then God told me to continue to prepare for there was more to come.

A very good friend and an elder in the church sought me out to say that he believed that I am called to fill my heart and mind with the ways that God's people can best prepare for what is to come, both spiritual as well as physical salvation. He acknowledged the fact that only the Lord can direct my thoughts, paths of inquiry, and desires for the welfare of His people. He told me to have faith, pray often, love well and as I feel God's spirit, I will have His direction. I was thirty-five years old.

During the year 2001, while I was still thirty five years old, the Lord God led me to an understanding of the guidelines on which I needed to focus on in His ministry. Those guidelines are unselfish true love, which is God. That love needs to work through us so we can give our lives for all those around us, for His Kingdom to come, and for His will to be done.

To sum up this condensed version of my life's testimony, I would like to say that it is true that God does not leave our side. Throughout my life I have fallen back and made many bad decisions, and yet He keeps on showing me ways back. I feel unworthy. I never totally left Him, but that is not enough. I need to continue to prepare and to stomp out those weaknesses that still plague me from time to time. It is up to me what my final destiny will be, and if that destiny is with God, there is no room for a hypocrite or the wicked. So, as I continue to strengthen my relationship with God through my Lord Jesus Christ, I understand that no one, man or woman, nor any organization or man-governed denomination on earth will get my family and me to everlasting salvation. It is my personal relationship with Him, combined with the strength of those brothers and sisters of the true restoration that will dictate whether or not I will see the Kingdom of God. It is through this awareness of my life experiences with the only two churches that exist, that will lead me to the understanding of His Everlasting Glory, and to the happiness that is meant for all of His creation.

"Thus speaketh Christ our Lord to us:

Ye call Me Master and obey Me not.
Ye call Me Light and see Me not,
Ye call Me Way and walk Me not,
Ye call Me Life and choose Me not,
Ye call Me Wise and follow Me not,
Ye call Me Fair and love Me not,
Ye call Me Rich and want Me not,
Ye call Me Eternal and seek Me not,
Ye call Me Nobel and serve Me not,
Ye call Me Gracious and trust Me not,
Ye call Me Might and honor Me not,
Ye call Me just and fear Me not,
If I condemn you, blame Me not."

An inscription on the cathedral in Lubeck, Germany.

Chapter Two
Communion Awareness

Prior to going to our congregations to partake in the sacrament, we should prepare prior to this communion. We should do this by prayer and fasting, asking for guidance and repenting of what we know is wrong in our lives. Then, after our participation in communion, we know we have a fresh start. But more often than not, we come to our congregations not with preparation, but to hear the messages. Then we look upon the messenger and critique his methods of preaching, or think of someone else the message might better fit, or even take offense that the message is directed toward us.

In this chapter I am going to specifically ask you to, in fact, take this message personally. It is specifically directed to you so that you critique ONLY your personal relationship and covenant with God. Look to only that which keeps you bound to the world and putting God off for some future time. Read this chapter as if your hearing this for the first time. Concentrate on the message itself.

    When we go to our congregation to partake in our Lord's last supper, we do it physically in remembrance of what Jesus did for us 2000+ years ago. But it shouldn't stop there. We must respond spiritually with acts of religious discipline. It is far easier to go through the motions physically and to superficially partake, than it is to spiritually prepare for days by fasting, praying and seeking His Kingdom. When we partake without proper preparation, we are skating on thin ice. We grow prideful in our man-governed denominations, thinking if we just attend and live life the best we can, that will be enough. I say to you that if we think this way, we are in danger of not being known by our Lord Jesus Christ.

    We must come to the knowledge of the importance of our spiritual preparation. This is done prior, during and after we partake of the emblems by truly acknowledging our wrongs and coming to God with more prayer, fasting and repentance. We need to meditate on what Jesus endured so that we might be filled with the Holy Ghost and be forgiven. We put the broken bread in our mouths in remembrance of His body and the time He was with man physically, knowing He allowed His body to be tortured for us. Then when we put the wine in our mouths, we also do this in remembrance of Him and the blood from that torture He endured. I know it is hard to hear the word "torture" because it is not a word we are used to in sermons. We have grown accustomed to hearing these phrases; "He shed His blood." and "He died for us." Because of this a lot of us become immune to the physical and spiritual aspects of what He had gone through.

It is ironic that I had to come back and add this paragraph because of Mel Gibson's movie "The Passion of the Christ," because this movie gave a realistic interpretation of the actual torture our Lord went through. This type of reality is what is missing in this horrible but true event. Just saying the phrases "He died for us" or "He shed his blood for us" does not give us the reality of His pain, physically, spiritually, or mentally.

The disciples partook of the emblems with the spirit of sincerity and sorrow picturing what Jesus told them would happen to Him; and, more importantly, actually lived during the time of the events.

In the four gospels we read that Jesus was bound. What

that does to one's circulation and the burns from the friction of that raw rope can not feel good. Then He was whipped by what many believe to be a cat of nine tails, a short whip with chips of metal at the end of each tail. To be whipped is frightfully painful and mentally exhausting. Were you ever punished with a belt as a child, or accidentally got hit with a jump rope? It hurts. If it hits hard enough, it brings welts; and if it hits harder still, it tears the skin, leaving an ongoing pain with every little move. Now put small pieces of metal in with that. The damage that it would do, and the pain that it would cause is just overwhelming. He was stripped, which humiliated Him. Then a nice robe was put on Him over the painful burns, welts, cuts and tears that hurt even more with something touching them. It adds to the ongoing pain, with every move. With this came a crown of thorns. Thorns! That's like long, dry, thick needles piercing and cutting the skin as it was smashed over Jesus' head. The sweat that had begun, I am sure, way before is now spilling into the wounds on His head and stinging as it had with the cuts and wounds from the bindings and whippings earlier. Now they again humiliated Him by mocking His sovereignty and spitting on Him. Scripture does not tell us how many soldiers are partaking in this activity, so the frequency of these events are anyone's guess. They then took a bamboo like reed and struck Him on the head with it. Again, the wounds from the ropes, whips, thorns and sweat have not stopped hurting as he is being hit on the head and on the crown with the reeds. Just think of the pain and endurance our Lord was going through.

As if that was not enough, He then was forced to carry a huge wooden cross a fair distance to His place of death. But remember the other wounds did not go away, in fact depending on the weight of the cross, it did more damage as its weight shifted back and forth over these wounds. When He fell, He was forced to pick it back up and continue. If there were any blisters formed or splinters received, we can only guess. When He reached Golgotha, He was forced to lie on the cross while the soldiers held Him down. That alone had to hurt His tired and worn limbs. They then took spikes and hammered each one through him. First they pierced the skin, then the muscle, and finally the other side into the cross itself. If that wasn't bad enough, they had to pound the nails further into the cross for stability. He felt the nail sliding through His flesh with each pound. This happened again with the other hand and then His feet. Remember the other wounds have not stopped hurting but instead intensified with each action.

It was still not over. They had to erect the cross. All that movement and change of gravity as His body was being shaken and lifted, and the pressures, and the further tearing had to be unbearable.

Was it over yet? No. He was then forced to hang there hurting, bleeding, tearing, and stinging for six more hours. Six hours! I can't even imagine standing in one place for one hour, let along hanging with excruciating pain for six hours. Then the sky darkened. Surely this was when it came to an end for Him. No. He hung there for three more hours! So, if I did the math correctly, this means that He hung there for nine hours before He committed His Spirit to the hands of God. The torture to his body was not over until they had pierced His side with a spear and watched his blood spill out.

After this graphic description, we see "torture" is a kind word when trying to find a term to use for God giving His only begotten Son for us. Now that we have the reality and extent of what Jesus endured for us pictured in our minds, know that this was the beginning of our personal salvation. Let me say that again, "our personal salvation." And it is taking place for us today, just as it did over 2000 years ago. This is so humbling because, when we truly look down deep at our own selves today, there are very few who would even attempt doing this for Him. But you see, this is what God's love is all about. We need to see how His love works. We need to come to an understanding that it is imperative that we love like that. The need to be like Him, not to become a god like Him but to become a loving creation of his, to allow Him to live in us. Understanding the weak state we are now in, we must say, "I'm sorry. Please forgive me. Please help me find my way."

We must first seek God and bring the admission of our sins, along with our repentance, so that He can transform our lives through our individual effort of seeking Him.

Now that we have our foundation set upon His rock, let us go to Colossians, chapter 3 to read what His Word says about what our transformation should be focusing on. Verses 1 and 2 read;

"If ye then be risen with Christ,
Seek those things which are above,
Where Christ sitteth on the right hand of
God, Set your affection on things above,
Not on things on the earth."

We must seek God first in all we do and use Him as our guide and learn to focus on what He wants us to do. Verse 3 states, **"For ye are dead, and your life is hid with Christ in God."** Somehow our lives, my life, is hidden with Jesus inside God. These are very important words to ponder. The next verse says, **"When Christ, who is our life, shall appear, then shall ye also appear with Him in glory."** If we are connected to Him, we are a part of His life. Ponder the question, "How are we connected with Him." Verse 5 explains, **"Mortify therefore your members which are upon the earth; fornication, uncleanness, inordinate affection, evil concupiscence (unlawful lust), and covetousness, which is idolatry;"**

    Mortify means to humble or restrain, and members are parts of your physical body, the flesh that is tempted. Verses 8 and 9 continue, "But now ye also put off all these; anger, wrath, malice, blasphemy, filthy communication out of your mouth. Lie not one to another, seeing that ye have put off the old man with his deeds;" These too we must restrain, if we fail we will see the wrath of God.

Verses 10 and 11 show we are all equal in Christ. "And have put on the new man, which is renewed in knowledge after the image of Him that created him; Barbarian, Scythian, bond nor free; but Christ is all, and in all."

In stopping these bad habits and seeking God, verse 12 tells us we will gain more knowledge; this is the new man. "Put on therefore, as the elect of God, holy and beloved, bowels of mercies, kindness, humbleness of mind, meekness, long suffering;"

We must develop these weapons of God within us if we are to be blessed. Verse 13 continues the list; "Forbearing one another, and forgiving one another, if any man have a quarrel against any; even as Christ forgave you, so also do ye." Forbearing is to be easy, mild and sympathetic. We must be kind to all those around us.

Verses 14 and 15 pronounce a blessing; **"And above all these things put on charity, which is the bond of perfectness. And let the peace of God rule in your hearts, to that which also ye are called in one body; and be thankful."** Charity and peace of God will have power in our hearts when we seek Him first in all things. Let me say that again, in all things. To seek, I believe, is to practice and focus upon His Word and relate it to our everyday Lifestyles.

Verses 17 and 18, **"And whatsoever ye do in word or deed, do all in the name of the Lord Jesus, giving thanks to God and the Father by him. Wives, submit yourselves unto your own husbands, as it is fit in the he Lord."** The Lord tells wives to submit unto their husbands, as it is fit in the Lord. The word submit means to defer, relinquish, and comply. But the best definition I found in a thesaurus was "to abide." This is the meaning that best fits the understanding of what Christ wants from us, to abide in Him. It is not asking wives to cower or be slaves, not in the least. It is asking for wives to become one with their husbands as we all are asked to become one with Christ.

Verse 19 says; **"Husbands, love your wives, and be not**

bitter against them." This means to love as Christ loves the church with compassion, charity, kindness, and forbearing. Again this is oneness that Christ is asking of us all. If the husbands misinterpret these words and become tyrants or bosses over their wives or if the wives misinterpret these words and take offense and fight against their meaning, then both will never grow as the Lord is asking, and we all lose. To grow as one. It is imperative that we grow in His love, which we will cover more in the next chapter.

Verse 20 continues, **"Children, obey your parents in all things; for this is well pleasing unto the Lord."** This is hard for them sometimes, but they must trust God's guidance. If their parents are wanting them to do a wrong such as stealing, murder, sex or things that are clearly against God's law, they should go to God in prayer and see what His guidance tells them. Children must remember that God is just and He will not steer them astray. However, children must also remember the importance of the fifth commandment which states that they should honor their mother and father. If they are asked or told to do something that may be seen as an attack against their pride or desires, they must realize that only they have the power to respond as God would have them do, because of their agency. Once this is instilled in them they will see a more desired path before them.

Verse 21 adds, **"Fathers, provoke not your children to anger, lest they be discouraged."** Provoking their anger will only trigger rebellion. I myself continued to do this to my daughters until I came to the understanding of this verse. Now, through repentance and fasting, I am better guided by God.

Verse 22, **"Servants, obey in all things your masters according to the flesh; not with eye-service, as men-pleaser; but in singleness of heart, fearing God."** This verse is often confused. It is not giving the OK to sin if our masters tell us to but is asking us to perform our work correctly and whole-heartedly and not be a "yes man" or do anything to be the bosses favorite. We can do our work with skill and confidence, knowing that our skills are but gifts from our Lord. This is respecting and fearing God, because to not do so is to not be truthful to who we are, and at the same time we know what is right and wrong because of our oneness of heart with God. This is why we cannot separate the laws of God from the laws of man. They have to go hand in hand.

Verse 23 cautions, "**And whatsoever ye do, do it heartily, as to the Lord, and not unto men;**" This again reiterates we are to work hard and be honest, and not to do things against the Word of God.

Finally, in verses 24 and 25, "**Knowing that of the Lord ye shall receive the reward of the inheritance; for ye serve the Lord Christ. But he that doeth wrong shall receive for the wrong which he had done: and there is no respect of person.**"

These are the things which we need to meditate on so that the transformation of our lives will be set in motion **BY GOD**. If we do not, it doesn't matter if we are high society, poor, middle class, strong, weak, black, white, republican, democrat, Catholic, or Baptists, or just doing the best we can and not bothering anyone; we will see His wrath just the same. It's all up to us as individuals and up to our personal covenants with Him.

Again I must add another paragraph in this chapter before I am done. By the time you finish this book it should be clear to you that I do not believe that there is one denomination out there that is the "right church" but that there are only but two churches, Gods and the devils as scripture tells us. But I do believe that the

Holy Bible is a collection of writings that was put together as a record of our God and Christ here on earth. A history given by those in the eastern hemisphere and are indeed holy and inspired writings. I also believe in the Book of Mormon that is a history given by those in the western hemisphere and are indeed holy and inspired writings. I am not a Mormon. I am not a Catholic. I am not a Baptist. But I am a Christian that believes there is no way to Heaven but through our Lord Jesus Christ. And when we read His scriptures we do not take away or change that which the Lord has given us. In the Book of Mormon in the book of Moroni, chapter four and five, there are two prayers that were given to say over the bread and the wine and nowhere else in scripture do we find these beautiful words; **"O God, the Eternal Father, We ask Thee in the name of Thy Son Jesus Christ to bless and sanctify this bread to the souls of all those who partake of it, That they may eat in remembrance of the body of Thy Son, and witness unto Thee, O God, the Eternal Father, That they are willing to take upon them the name of Thy Son, and always remember Him and keep His commandments which He hath given them, That they may always have His Spirit to be with them. Amen."**

and " O God, the Eternal Father, We ask Thee in the name of Thy Son Jesus Christ to bless and sanctify this wine to the souls of all those who drink of it, That they may do it in remembrance of the blood of Thy Son which was shed for them, That they may witness unto Thee, O God, the Eternal Father, That they do always remember Him, That they may have His Spirit to be with them. Amen. These prayers were given as a reminder of the path He has prepared for us. That we do not fall away from the purpose He has for His creation. But there are some now that want to take away the words of scripture to be more conforming to man governed society and its political correctness that is deceiving and eroding the foundation He has laid down before us. One of the very denominations that once believed in the Book of Mormon are slowly taking away from its fullness to compromise with man's authority and prideful way of life by making it their denominational law to not read these prayers from scripture anymore but to take out the "Eternal Father" so as to make it less gender specific. This is sad and we must not allow ourselves to be pulled into this selfish mindset of society.

In closing this chapter I would like to share a type and

shadow. When my daughters were young their Uncle Orban, my brother-in-law, made up a game with them, and now all of our family plays this game with all our young family members. He would be clear on the other side of a room or the other side of the yard, and he would stretch his arms out as wide as they would go. Then he would say to my daughters, one at a time, of course, "You better hurry. They are closing!" While he was slowly closing his arms, my daughter would pretend that she was not paying attention, but in reality she was hearing every word. Then at the last possible second, as Uncle Orban was closing his arms, she would make a mad dash and slam into his chest for safety and a big hug. Then sometimes when one daughter, son, niece, or nephew did not want to play or waited to long, he would call out to another to see if he or she could make it.

    I bring this up because the Lord our God did come to earth, did go through a horrible torture, and spilled His blood for us, each one, so that we might hear His Words and come unto His Body. He is hoping that we do not grow away from Him. He is hoping that we stop pretending we do not hear. He is hoping that we do not wait too long to make a mad dash to be in the safety of His arms. Some will and some will not reach that safety. Remember, when we go to communion, Jesus' arms are stretched out wide and he is saying to you;

"They are closing."

"Hereby know we that we dwell in Him, and He in us, because He hath given us of His Spirit."

> ~I John 4:13, I.V.

Chapter Three
The Four Garden Tools

My wife and I love to garden. During the spring and summer it is hard to catch us anywhere but in our yard, during our off time, doing some kind of gardening; whether it is building a gazebo, or planting flowers and trees around it, or just watering and enjoying the peace we have in our yard. One beautiful day, after I had just finished a trellis and wanted to put some kind of saying on it, I asked Maria to close her eyes and feel the warmth of the sun on her face and the cool breeze and then tell me in one sentence what she was feeling. She did, paused for a minute or so, then smiled and said; "Shhhh, listen. God's calling." It's not what she was hearing but it put into words what she was feeling. So, with that wonderful experience she just relayed to me, I decided that was the exact sentence to put on the trellis.

Throughout scripture there are lots of references to gardening, planting the seeds, cultivating, pulling out the tares, etc. Well, this got me thinking and pondering more about the parable of the sower. It seemed there was a lot of gardening going on, but with what tools? As I read this parable over many times and studied it, I found that by using garden tools as *analogies* for the meaning of this parable, I began to discover a wondrous meaning. This chapter covers four things I will consider to be those tools. But remember these tools I use are from the authors efforts to define what they were interpreting within themselves as they related with the Holy Spirit. Jesus tells us in Mark, chapter 12, that our God is one Lord, and that we should love the Lord God with all of our heart, soul, mind and strength. He tells us that this is the first commandment and that the second is that we should love our neighbor as ourselves. There are no commandments greater.

How do we love with all four of these tools? Two seem to be only labels of basically non-tangible objects, one an organ we do not really have control over and one defines how strong we are. Before we look at these four tools we must first need to understand what love is, so we will know what we are to do with our heart, soul, mind and strength. Once we understand what love is, we can learn how to use our four newly found tools. If we do not know what love is, then we cannot love God or anything with true understanding. That would be like running a marathon without even knowing what running is. The scriptures are very clear, and we must study to know this truth. Scriptures tell us that God is Love. 1 John 4:7-8 states; **"Beloved, let us love one another; for love is of God; and every one that loveth is born of God, and knoweth God. He that loveth not knoweth not God; for God is love."**

  I hear good sermons all the time which tell us that God is loving, and their interpretation of this scripture just explains how loving God is, and that He is not really the emotion of love. But the Word said, "love is OF "God," not FROM God, or TO God, but *OF* God. Then John continues in verse 9, **"In this was manifested the love of God toward us, Because that God sent his only begotten Son into the world that we might live through Him."** Then later in verse 16 we read, **"And we have known and believed the love that God hath to us, God is love; and he that dwelleth in love dwelleth in God, and God in him."** Here we see that he says they have known and believed that God *IS* love. Notice how the first sentence is translated "...that God hath to us," not hath given to us, or hath brought to us, but "hath to us." He is to us Love, and we dwell in Him and He in us because of it.

So if God is Love and Love is God, when we feel something telling us that we love someone, we are in a sense *Goding* that person. By understanding that God is Love, and understanding we use love as a verb (action word); we, in fact, use God to know God. This is not taking away at all what God is. I am not saying God is an emotion we feel. I am saying the emotion we feel, as love, is God's presence in us. So when we extend this knowledge to our neighbors, we are sharing how we use God the verb to know God the noun. We are exercising His spiritual presence in order to feel His physical presence. This process is simple once the understanding of it is mastered, and it becomes a continuous act of charity that is Love the verb which source is Love the noun, God. Summarizing it simply, God is in and through all things, and His presence within all things is the love all things experience within themselves, if in fact they can feel. In Romans 13:10 we read, **"Love worketh no ill to his neighbor; therefore Love is the fulfilling of the law."** What law? The Spiritual Law, The Holy Ghost, The Three in One, God;

God is Love and Love is the Law. Now lets take a deeper look at the four tools Jesus gave to cultivate this love within us.

The Heart

Not long before I wrote this, a pastor was teaching a class and mentioned the time when Jesus cursed a tree for not bearing fruit. We discussed how this tree could represent us, and when we do not produce fruit, we too would be cursed. Let's use this example as an introduction to this topic of the heart being used as a tool. Let's go to Luke 6:45 where the Word says, **"A good man out of the treasure of his heart, bringeth forth that which is good. And an evil man out of the evil treasure of his heart, bringeth forth that which is evil; for of the abundance of the heart his mouth speaketh."** If we do not become aware of the spiritual nature of our hearts, then the world or society will consume them with the cold and darkness of selfishness. This selfishness becomes our vale of blindness that is self-satisfaction. This spiritual awareness is the basic foundation for successfully loving God and using all of our heart. Most importantly, we use our agency in choosing to understand this foundational principal. We read in 2 Nephi 3;28-30 in the Book of Mormon,

"And upon these I write the things of my soul and many of the scriptures which are engraven upon the plates of brass, for my soul delighteth in the scriptures, and my heart pondereth them and writeth them for the learning and the profit of my children; Behold, my soul delighteth in the things of the Lord, and my heart pondereth continually upon the things which I have seen and heard."

Our heart thinks? Not in the same way as our minds, but through the discernment of right and wrong, light and dark, and good and evil. The heart ponders with sensitivity to feelings and with a communication through awareness of the Spirit. When we think about it, we can remember weighty feelings at times when we were in need or troubles, and at other times we felt a lifting of that weight when we were freed of something. Like when I was a boy doing my paper route that I shared earlier in my testimony, or the time I helped my mother in the fire. What is this awareness? Nephi continues in 2 Nephi chapter 3 versus 31-34,

"Nevertheless, notwithstanding the great goodness of the Lord in showing me His great and marvelous works, My heart exclaimeth, O wretched man that I am! Yea, my heart sorroweth because of my flesh, My soul grieveth because of mine iniquities; I am encompassed about because of the temptations and the sins which   doth so easily beset me; And when I desire to rejoice, my heart groaneth because of my sins."

This is communication and discernment at its best. Nephi is using action words like exclaim, sorrowful, and groaning to describe his heart. We also read in 1 Samuel 24:5 that David's heart smote him, and 1 Chronicles says, "let the heart of them rejoice," and again in Luke 2:19 it states, "Mary kept all these things and pondered them in her heart." Our hearts today are no different, and it is our agency that separates our hearts from our actions. If we lose control through deceit and slothfulness, then societal norms will have power over our hearts. When this happens to our agency, we chose to go with the flow. We are slothful, and slothfulness creates covetness, and covetness spawns selfishness. These behaviors lead our hearts to store up treasures of selfishness, which is evil.

In Moroni 8:29 in the Book of Mormon we are given an outline for success. We are all in the midst of this today as individuals, as a fellowship, and as a church.

"And the first fruits of repentance is baptism, and baptism cometh by faith, unto the fulfilling of the commandments, and the fulfilling of the commandments bringeth remission of sins, and the remission of sins bringeth meekness and lowliness of heart, and because of the meekness and lowliness of heart, comes the visitation of the Holy Ghost, which comforter filleth with hope and perfect love, which love endureth by diligence unto prayer, until the end shall come when all the saints shall dwell with God."

I believe that, as a people, there are very few of us that are past the "baptism cometh by faith" stage. This is not because we have no faith, but because we do not understand how to use the tool of the heart. Proverbs 2:2 tells us to "apply thine heart to understanding." That is why it is so difficult to fulfill the commandments, and therefore, because of this continual struggle, our remission from sins becomes stalled due to the slothfulness of our behavior. Why else do so many feel the continual need for repentance? Because a lot of us have not yet reached that form of spiritually understanding with the heart. We must know the origin of that loving feeling, which is the force which created us, God, within us. He communicates His existence within our hearts.

We read in Romans chapter 6 verse 17, **"But God be thanked, that ye are not the servants of sin, for ye have obeyed from the heart that form of doctrine which was delivered you."** Does the Word of God tell us to obey our hearts? No, the Word of God says that we must obey FROM the heart. We must use the heart as a tool to obey with. And we obey by following the Law, or Love, which is a form of doctrine that is in the heart. Brothers and Sisters, He is not far from each one of us (Acts 17:27). Seek Him by being aware of His presence. Feel Him by communicating with Him. We must not let the devil's influences of pride stand in the way of our purpose, the purpose God has for us. If we do, before we know it Brothers and Sisters, our procrastination will lead to our judgment. In closing of this section, let us understand these words by Moroni;

"Behold, I would exhort you that when ye shall read these things–if it be wisdom in God that ye should read them–That ye would remember how merciful the lord hath been unto the

children of men from the creation of Adam, even down until the time that ye shall receive these things, And ponder it in your hearts. And when Ye shall receive these things, I would exhort you that ye would ask God the Eternal Father, in the name of Christ, if these things are not true; And if ye shall ask with a sincere heart, with real intent, having faith in Christ, and He will manifest the truth of it unto you by the power of the Holy Ghost; And by the power of the Holy Ghost, ye may know the truth of all thing; And whatsoever thing is good, it just and true; Wherefore, nothing that is good denieth the Christ, but acknowledgeth that He is. And ye may know that He is by the power of the Holy Ghost; Wherefore, I would exhort you that ye deny not the power of God; for he worketh by power according to the faith of the children of men, the same today, tomorrow and forever."

  We have already read what Jesus told us about the first and second greatest commandments. We learned through this scripture that we must love God with the four tools which He has given us: the heart, soul, mind and strength. First we came to an understanding that God is love, and we must use our awareness of Him within ourselves by using our hearts to ponder with . If we do not, the world will cause our ability to have this spiritual communication of God to wax cold. After we become aware of this communication with our heavenly Father, and after we become aware of His presence within us through the pondering of our hearts, what then? That is where the second tool comes into our understanding.

The Soul

The second tool that Jesus spoke of is the soul, to love God with all of our soul. We now know God is Love and our heart is a physical organ that somehow spiritually ponders or discerns good and evil, but what is our soul? We first hear of our souls in Genesis chapter 2 when the Word says, **"And I the Lord God, formed man of the dust of the ground, and breathed into his nostrils the breath of life; and man became a living soul."**

Here God formed man from the earth, but man was not yet a living being or soul. It wasn't until God took something from Himself, his breath, and physically routed this breath into the earthly dust form. This very act caused the one formed of God to become living flesh, creation with the living soul. A spiritual/physical metamorphosis, if you will. He has told us that all things were already created spiritually by His Word, but it wasn't until this verse that a living soul, with the coming together of body and spirit, had its start. In the Inspired Version of the Bible, Genesis 6:61 states,

"Therefore I give unto you a commandment, to teach these things freely unto your children, saying, that by reason of transgression cometh the fall, which fall bringeth death; and inasmuch as ye were born into the world by water and blood, and the spirit, which I have made, and so become of dust a living soul."

The beauty of this is the dust form combining with God's breath, only happened once that we know of, with Adam. Since then flesh had already been created, so that now in the blood and water, within the flesh, life begins, and sometime in this process God continues to create living souls by adding spirit. Other scripture says that after a soul is created, it cannot be destroyed.

"Therefore as the soul could never die, and that fall had brought upon all mankind a spiritual death as well as a temporal–that is, they were cut off from the presence of the Lord–therefore, it was expedient that mankind should be reclaimed from this spiritual death; therefore, as they had become carnal, sensual and devilish by nature, this probationary state became a state for them to prepare. It became a preparatory state. And now remember, my son, if it were not for the plan of redemption laying it aside—As soon as they were dead, their souls were miserable, being cut off from the Lord." (Alma 19:90-92)

Let's sum up what we are saying about the soul. The living soul is a spirit created with some connection to flesh, or in other words the spirit is woven with the flesh to make the soul. To not focus on, or love God, through our hearts and souls is to distance ourselves from God, thus making our hearts vulnerable to wax cold by the world's influences, and which starves our souls. Now we start to see this connection between the heart and soul; the heart is flesh, and the soul is made of spirit and flesh that has a connection with man's first flesh, Adam.

God's breath + earth dust form = Adam + bone from side = Eve + Adam + breath = descendants. Souls. You. Me. Etc. Confusing, I know but clear in God's sight, and someday science will catch up and understand as well.

The soul belongs to God. Your soul, my soul, all souls

are God's for He created them. In Ezekiel 18:4 we read, "Behold, all souls are mine; as the soul of the father, so also the soul of the son in mine; the soul that sinneth, shall die."

This dying is a spiritual death, or a being cut off from God. This means we belong to God, and what we do with ourselves determines our eternal life. "**And it is given unto them to know good from evil; wherefore, they are agents unto themselves. "** (Genesis 6:58) So the good side to this is that we just direct our hearts and souls toward God and hold fast to His commandments to love Him, we will meet Him in eternity.

"I glory in plainness! I glory in truth! I glory in my Jesus, for he hath redeemed my soul from hell! I have charity for my people, and great faith in Christ that I shall meet many souls spotless of His judgment seat." (2 Nephi 15:7-8)

In Mark chapter 8 verses 38-40: "But whosoever shall be willing to lose his life for My sake, and the gospel, the same shall save it. For what shall it profit a man if he shall gain the whole world, and lose his own soul? Therefore deny yourselves of these, and be not ashamed of Me."

Our heart ponders spiritual awareness through feelings

and emotions. Our soul absorbs our spiritual acceptance of the presence of Love or God. Our soul is a tool that thirsts, therefore it is like a sponge, it needs to be filled. David's Psalm 63 beautifully touches on this awareness,

"O God, thou are my God; early will I seek thee; my soul thirsteth for Thee. My flesh longeth for Thee in a dry and thirsty land, where no water is; to see Thy power and Thy glory, so as I have been Thee in the sanctuary. Because Thy loving-kindness is better than life, my lips shall praise Thee. Thus will I bless Thee while I live; I will lift up my hands in Thy name. My soul shall be satisfied as with marrow and fatness; and my mouth shall praise Thee with joyful lips; When I remember Thee on my bed, and meditate on the in the night watches. Because Thou hast been my help, therefore in the shadow of Thy wings will I rejoice. My soul followeth hard after Thee; Thy right hand upholdeth me. But those that seek my soul, to destroy it, shall go into the lower parts of the earth. They shall fall by the sword; they shall be a portion for the foxes. But the king shall rejoice in God; every one that sweareth by Him shall glory; but the mouth of them that speak lies shall be stopped."

The soul needs to be filled. To go against God, or turn away from Him and His word, is to starve the soul. Choosing to do that which the heart feels to be unrighteous turns the heart cold, breaking the connection between our heart and soul, and that starves the soul of the Love of God. This in turn distances us from a personal relationship with God. 2 Nephi 11:117-121 states,

"...when that day shall come, they shall be visited of the Lord of Hosts, with thunder and with earthquake, and with a great noise, and with storm and tempest, and with the flame of devouring fire; And all the nations that fight against Zion and that distress her shall be as a dream of a night vision; Yea, it shall be unto them even as unto a hungry man which dreameth, and behold—he eatedth, But he awaketh, and his soul is empty; Or like unto a thirsty man who dreameth, and behold, he drinketh, but he awaketh, and behold his is faint and his soul hath appetite; Yea, even so shall the multitude of all the nations be that fight against Mount Zion."

This seems to speak of filling the soul for salvation, but it is our awareness and our direction of agency that will put our soul in a position to be filled. In Joshua 22:5 Moses charges us to serve God with all of our hearts and all of our souls. "To serve" is to use our agency in directing our souls to Him from our hearts in order to be filled with His Spirit. Our soul is a tool we must use to store God's Spirit and to strengthen our connection to our eternity. God's direction is to love Him. In Deuteronomy 10:12-13 we read,

"And now, Israel, what doth the Lord thy God require of thee, but to fear the Lord thy God, to walk in all His ways, and to love Him, and to serve the Lord thy God with all thy heart and with all thy soul, to keep the commandments of the Lord, and His statutes, which I command thee this day for thy good."

In Isaiah 55:3 we again see another promise that relates to this connection with God, "Incline your ear, and come unto me; hear, and your soul shall life; and I will make an everlasting covenant with you, even the sure mercies of David."

Hearing Him is the awareness we talked about earlier, and this awareness is important in our relationship with Him. In closing this section of the chapter, I want to say when we feel guilty, revengeful, angry, etc. because of our weakness or shortcomings; or when we feel we do not deserve to go to our congregation, or pray, or practice our righteousness, we distance our soul from the ability to be filled with God's Spirit. Then our heart suffers emotionally and, aided by the world, it waxes cold. It isn't until we sincerely begin to love God and to go to Him in prayer and study the Word that our soul begins to be filled.

We now know our hearts work as an identifier of good and evil. It does this through pondering or discerning the difference between the two, and this is communication with the presence of God through His spiritual connection within our flesh. We know our soul, made of flesh and spirit, thirsts to be filled with the Holy Ghost to seal its salvation in eternity. So the soul absorbs that which the heart spiritually accepts of God's love, and if the heart turns away from His love, the soul starves and is cut off from God.

Now comes the question, what makes the decision for the direction of the heart? The answer is,

<u>The Mind</u>

In Genesis 23:7 Abraham states to the children of Heth, "if it be your mind..." It seems to me that the word mind is a term used for decision. But what makes this different from the heart's pondering? Doesn't that make the heart deciding and not the mind? No. As we said earlier, the heart identifies good and evil, but it is the mind that decides upon action of that identification. In Romans 7:24-27 it says,

"And now I see another law, even the commandment of Christ, and it is imprinted in my mind. But my members are warring against the law of my mind, and bringing me into captivity to the law of sin which is in my members. And if I subdue not the sin which is in me, but with the flesh serve the law of sin; O wretched man that I am! Who shall deliver me from the body of this death? I thank God through Jesus Christ our Lord, then, that so with the mind I myself serve the law of God."

As we stated earlier this serving the law of God is done with our agency, and our agency is done with the mind against the other fleshly members of the body. Why? Because the gift of decision is given to our minds. The other members of the body only deal with sensations of feelings, spirit, and emotions. When we begin to give into these self-satisfying sensations, we give power to them, and we begin to grow selfish. This selfishness then isolates us from God and His Holy Spirit. The Lord gives a parable of two adulterers in Ezekiel 23:17-18, 22, & 28 illustrating that our minds can be alienated from God, by our poor choices.

"And the Babylonians came to her into the bed of love, and they defiled her with their whoredom, and she was polluted with them, and her mind was alienated from me by them. So she discovered her whoredoms, and discovered her nakedness; then my mind was alienated from her, like as my mind was alienated from her sister. ...I will raise up thy lovers against thee, by whom thy mind is alienated from me, and I will bring them against thee on every side. ...into the hand of them by whom thy mind is alienated."

So is that it? The mind deciphers the good and evil pondering of the heart and chooses good over evil? No. It is not that easy. For without the Law being imprinted on our minds, we will not be able to resist the strength of our other members' sensations, because the mind can be doubtful, as we read in Luke 12:31, and it also ponders along with the heart, as we read in Luke 1:29. So how then do we get the law imprinted on our minds? We must first renew our minds as it states in Ephesians 4:22-24,

71

"And now I speak unto you concerning the former conversation, by exhortation, that ye put off the old man, which is corrupt according to the deceitful lusts; and be renewed in the mind of the Spirit; and that ye put on the new man, which after God is created in righteousness and true holiness."

We cannot give place for the adversary as it says in verse 27 of this same chapter of Ephesians; And from verse 28-32 we see a list of renewal,

"If you steal, steal no more. Don't talk corruption any longer to tear anyone down, but stay positive in your thinking and edify others by finding that which is good, focus not on their weaknesses but their strengths. This will show others God's grace in you. By not being sad or angry at God's law will renew your covenant with Him. Make sure all negativity is ignored within you so you can always be kind to one another. You must be tender hearted, forgiving means forgetting. This is the Law of God. Even as God has forgiven and forgotten your sins."

This will renew your mind and ready it for receiving God's Word through reading and studying scripture as Acts 17:11 shows, "These were more noble than those in Thessalonica, in that they received the word with all readiness of mind and searched the scriptures daily whether those things were so." But as in Acts 17:27, we must be willing to find Him, "That they should seek the Lord, if they are willing to find Him, for He is not far from every one of us."

    The willingness of mind is fueled by our souls thirst to be filled by God's Spirit, but it can only be directed to do so by our agency. Once these are accomplished, then our faith grows and the law begins to be imprinted on our minds. Then a great thing happens, God begins to stir up our minds through remembrance of that which is embedded there. This stirring up of our minds is repeated throughout scripture as we in turn want to stir the minds of others as in II Peter 3:1-4 below,

    "This second epistle, beloved, I now write unto you; in which I stir up your pure minds by way of remembrance; that ye may be mindful of the words which were spoken before by the holy prophets, and of the commandments of us, the apostles of the Lord and Savior; Knowing the first, that in the days that shall come scoffers, walking after their own lusts."

    By renewing our minds, as we stated earlier, we bring to

light the covenant that is spoke of in Hebrews 8:10, **"For this is the covenant that I will make with the house of Israel after those days, saith the Lord; I will put my laws into their mind, and write them in their hearts; and I will be to them a God, and they shall be to me a people."**

Again the heart and mind work together to feed the soul; if the mind is willing, and if the mind is spiritual. We see in 1 Corinthians 2:14-16 what happens when we let the natural run our life rather than the spiritual, meaning the members of the body that are warring against the mind versus God's law being imprinted on our minds. **"But the natural man receiveth not the things of the Spirit of God; for they are foolishness unto him; neither can he know them, yet he himself is judged of no man. For who hath known the mind of the Lord, that he may instruct him? But we have the mind of Christ."**

We must understand, to become closer to God, we have to understand the awareness of these four tools and their purposes. By doing this we become spiritual. We read in Romans 8:4-8,

> **"That the righteousness of the law might be fulfilled in us,**

who walk not after the flesh, but after the Spirit. For they that are after the flesh do mind the things of the flesh: but they that are after the Spirit, the things of Spirit. For to be carnally minded in death; but to be spiritually minded is life and peace. Because the carnal mind is enmity against God; for it is not subject to the law of God, neither indeed can be. So then they that are after the flesh cannot please God."

Using our four tools or gifts, as we have talked about, is being righteous in the Spirit, and being righteous in the Spirit is being spiritually minded. So to allow the physical self-satisfying members to take control of our decisions is to be carnally minded, and enmity means to be hostile, so being carnally minded is being hostile against God, which will starve our souls. So we must stay focused on Him. Be sure to pray for understanding, ask God to open the doors of salvation. We must become lowly in mind as Philippians 2:1-8 speaks of and serve the Lord with humility of mind, as Acts 20:19 points out. In closing this part, let us imprint two more verses of scripture to our minds. Isaiah 26:3 states, "Thou wilt keep him in perfect peace, whose mind is stayed on thee; because he trusteth in thee." And II

Timothy 1:7 states, **"For God hath not given us the spirit of fear; but the power of love, and of a sound mind."** Ahhh, now for the area we all, from time to time, wish we had an abundance of.

<u>The Strength</u>

We have the heart that discerns between good and evil, and our soul that needs to be filled with the Holy Spirit of God, and our mind that makes that choice of direction so that our soul can be filled and we will have everlasting understanding. That is becoming easy to see and hear now, but we must actually have the strength to make the correct choices in the first place. Where does this strength come from? Why isn't our saying, "I have faith" good enough?

After the Lord delivered him from the hands of his enemies Paul wrote in Psalms 18:2, **"The Lord is my rock and my fortress, and my deliverer; my God, my strength, in whom I will trust; my buckler, and the horn of my salvation, and my high tower."**

He said the Lord was his strength and later we read in Romans 7:24-27, **"...But my members are warring against the law of my mind, and bringing me into captivity to the law of sin which** is in my members..."

This clearly shows what we already know, that our members are in conflict with the law of the mind, and our strength is that force we recognize when we can overcome a weakness. Paul is telling us that God is that Strength. He is that Force. But there we go again, that is easy to see and hear, but how do we get it to use when we need it? First we have to be given it. Paul tells us in Psalms 29:11 that, "...**the Lord will give strength to his people...**" Alright. So who are His people? His people are those who believe in Him, repent of their sins, and are baptized in water and of the Holy Ghost. These are they who are His people. Then why is it so hard for us to receive the strength if all these areas are accomplished? Because it does not stop there. We must come to an understanding of His Love and then learn how to use His love to work through us, for our salvation and His sovereignty. In Romans chapter 5 we read that Christ died for our sins. God sent His only begotten Son to show us His example of how we can be in touch with the great love of God, which is God, and this happens when we choose to allow Him to work through us--for us.

This Love is what is so important. God loves us so much and we are so precious to Him that Jesus not only gave us the example and taught us lessons, but He allowed Himself to be tortured for the sins that we committed yesterday, today and will commit tomorrow. It isn't until we come to that understanding of His grace for us, that the awareness of this gift of strength becomes more clear.

In Ephesians chapter 4 we learn that the more we become righteous in His understanding, the more He will reveal Himself to us and the more we become the members of the Body of Christ. John 1 tells us that in the beginning was the Word. And in 1:14 he says, **"And the same word has made flesh, and dwelt among us, and we beheld his glory, the glory as of the Only Begotten of the Father, full of grace and truth."** Here we see scripture telling us that the Word is also Christ, the same that you read about. The same that scripture says is in us. In John chapter 5 Jesus says;

"...And the Father himself who hath sent me, hath borne witness of me. And verily I testify unto you, that ye have never heard his voice at any time, nor seen his shape; for ye have not his word abiding in you; and him who he hath sent, ye believe not. Search the scripture; for in them ye think ye have eternal life; and they are they which testify of me. And ye will not come to me that ye might have life, lest ye should honor me. I receive not honor from men. But I know you, that ye have not the love of God in you. How can ye believe, who seek honor one of another, and seek not the honor which cometh from God only? But if ye believe not his writings, how shall we believe my words?"

Here Jesus says that just because we read the scriptures and hear the truth, it does not mean that we actually understand them. We must be able to read the Scripture/Word/Christ and then ponder on its meaning. Then take it to God in prayer and faith so that He will show us its meaning. This process of worship and seeking Him in understanding will strengthen our relationship with God, and in turn we will receive strength and understanding from him, because of our practicing His will. Again I want to reiterate the fact that it is not just the reading of the words but the study of them, because it is through study and prayer that we find God. Corinthians 4:20, **"For the kingdom of God is not in word, but in power."** And the power is strength and it comes from when we use our agency to study and fast about what we read in the Word. In other words, it's our action to seek Him that brings the strength to us and that is powerful. This understanding brings us to Galatians 6:5-8,

"For every man shall bear his own burden. Let him that is taught in the word communicate unto him that teacheth in all good things. Be not deceived; God is not mocked; for whatsoever a man soweth, that shall he also reap. For he that soweth to his flesh shall of the

flesh reap corruption; but he that soweth to the Spirit shall of the Spirit reap life everlasting."

God wants us to understand and feel His Spirit as much as one who would understand that he must run to get into shape, or train for a career. The temptations of the flesh, (things that feel good to us physically like junk food, laziness, adultery, gambling, drunkenness, etc.) can be overcome through fasting, praying, and actively seeking him which is like sowing to the Spirit, and in that we will find everlasting life. This is when we receive our strength to do the things God wants us to do.

Now is when we can look at our garden tools and put

together how, in fact, Jesus tells us to receive the fullness of Christ and establish His Kingdom here on earth as it is in Heaven.

"And Jesus answered him, the first of all the commandments is: Hearken, and hear O Israel; The Lord our God is one Lord; and thou shalt love the Lord thy God with all thy heart, and with all thy soul. and with all thy mind, and with all thy strength. This is the first commandment. And the second is like this, Thou shalt love they neighbor as thyself. There is none other commandment greater than these."

With this scripture we can now see the four different tools at work doing four different things, but all four are being used simultaneously, all helping the other, and all spiritually connected by God's Holy Power. The heart ponders and discerns between good and evil. The soul yearns for God and collects the good that the heart accepts. The mind is the agency that chooses between the good and evil so that the heart can accept and the strength is that which God gives us when we seek Him in word and in all that we do, and this fills the mind so His law can be imprinted there.

Complicated as this might sound, it is powerful how this blessing of the Lord works with each individual, and this very blessing is being placed on so many at the same time, forming the body of Christ, His Church. My father-in-law, Ken Tousley, called this the *"Eternal Triangle,"* God, Me, and my neighbor.

Another scripture that gives four guidelines to assist the passage in Mark, is taken from Psalms 1:1-2, **"Blessed is the man that walketh not in the counsel of the ungodly, nor standeth in the way of sinners, nor sitteth in the seat of the scornful, But his delight is in t he law of the Lord: and in his law doth he meditate day and night."** And in verse 3 we see that which we reap because of it; **"And he shall be like a tree planted by the rivers of water, that bringeth fourth his fruit in his season; his leave also shall not wither; and whatsoever he doeth shall prosper."**

"The greatest pleasure I know is to do a good action by stealth, and to have it found out by accident."

~Charles Lamb

Chapter Four
Living the Church

"Ye have heard that it hath been said, thou shalt love thy neighbor, and hate thine enemy. But I say unto you; Love your enemies; bless them that curse you; do good to them that hate you; and pray for them that despitefully use you and persecute you; That ye may be the children of your Father who is in heaven; for he maketh his sun to rise on the evil and on the good, and sendeth rain on the just and the unjust. For if ye love only them which love you, what reward have you? Do not even the publicans the same? And if ye salute your brethren only, what do ye more than others? Do not even the publicans the same? Ye are therefore commanded to be perfect, even as your Father who is in heaven is perfect."

When I was a boy I very much looked up to my father. He was a hard man with a very strict military personality. But dad was honest and truthful, and I was drawn to that. I understood that I was not as strong as my father, but I worked hard trying to make him proud of me by being strong away from him and toward others. But when I was around my father, I became timid and humble. This was frustrating for me as a boy, and later as a man.

Then one day, when I was still a teenager, I found another man that was also a role model to me. But this man was quite different. He was a man of God. This man of God was gentle and kind, and I related well to his personality. But again, I tried hard to make this man proud of me because I knew that I was not as good as he. I worked hard studying and due to this, tried to understand the scriptures.

So my first two teachers in life one strong, straight forward, spoke what was on his mind, a type of mans man in society, and the other a patient, quiet, compassionate man of God. I have several times throughout my life compared the two to John Wayne and Jimmy Stewart.

Then one day when I was still a young man, I realized that my father did not yet know God as his personal savior, and I knew that I must try to share what I was finding out about God, so my father could be saved; but that never happened. One day while traveling with my dad in the car, I got up the courage to talk to him about this when he began to ridicule my twin brother's efforts in doing the same thing while my father visited him. I just clamed up and listened. I was too timid around him, and I kept procrastinating until it was too late. My father died a few years later.

The procrastination continued, and again it was too late for the man of God to see me reach my calling into the priesthood, because he too died. I did not begin to become consistent in my study of the scripture until after my father-in-law's death. This is a reality that slaps me in the face. In our surroundings today we see so many decisions to be made. What is moral vs. what is immoral, how to act with family vs. how to act in society, what political party to be with vs. our faith, what is funny, vs. what is sad, activates we enjoy vs. those things we do that we know are wrong.

My above story is sad but true. My father was John E. Cummings and the man of God was my father-in-law, Ken W. Tousley. The only reason those things happened the way they did was because I had not yet understood how to "live in His

Church." Life without God's governing power is life in the devil's church.

Someone once told me that God created us to have agency so that we can establish and govern the church. I disagree if that means we decide how to govern, and we decide what is good and moral from our sovereignty. God created us to fulfill His sovereignty over His creation and His earth, not so we can rule or use our power over the church. It means we use our agency to understand and allow God to govern through us. This act is making allowance for our knowledge of His Law of Love, to work with our agency to govern our lives so His Church can be established by Him. So, when someone hears the Word of God and knows what He teaches and then distorts this understanding to their own power to govern, they take away from God what is rightfully His, His Sovereignty. Not because God is weaker, but because we have our agency, and we have to learn and to be able to use our agency to seek His Kingdom. We cannot hear the gospel and believe it is us who are the authority and pass it off as our own.

It's like Mr. Tate in the old TV. sit-com Bewitched. He

was a boss in an advertising agency, and his number one brain was an employee named Darren Stevens. When an advertisement was being produced for a client, Darren would come up with these really good ideas and tell his boss, Mr. Tate. Tate would then try and understand the idea and then take it to the client as his own, always with the non-approval of Darren. When Christians, priesthood, and denominations do this, they either stand in limbo of spiritual growth or become false teachers that conform to society.

Another good example of this kind of error related path is something I heard that was said back in August 1852 when the leader of the Mormons, Brigham Young, preached publicly something to the effect of; "I shall see the time with yourselves that we shall know how to prepare to organize an earth like this one..." and that he goes on to preach that we all will become gods ourselves, equal to God, to rule over worlds like ours. If this is true of his preaching then that kind of lost path is what we will find ourselves in if we take away from God's sovereignty and claim it as ours. This is evil, and our agency must allow God's sovereignty in our lives and allow Him to govern through us, for us. Again, remember the two greatest commandments according to Jesus. Let's look at what Paul writes in Ephesians chapter 4 and see how we do this "allowing" with our agency so that we might be of one body--one spirit--one hope--one faith--and one baptism. This focus on God's love is His establishing His Church. **"I therefore, the prisoner of the Lord, beseech you that ye walk worthy of the vocation wherewith ye are called,"**

Vocation is your career or work that God has for you to do . To make ourselves worthy, we must focus on His Word to guide us. **"With all lowliness and meekness, with long-suffering, forbearing one another in love;"** Be calm and mild through transgressions done against us, dealing with all around you in the love that Jesus showed us as an example.

"Endeavoring to keep the unity of the Spirit in the bond of peace," Bond is the relationship we are constantly trying to strengthen with Christ. **"In one body, and one Spirit, even as ye are calling in one hope of your calling,"** Again, see how strengthening our personal relationship with God creates one body and one Spirit in Christ? We are called in one hope of our calling. Who is doing the hoping here? The body of Christ. The one Spirit that connects all who come to Him in peace and a contrite heart.

"One Lord, one faith, one baptism, one God and Father of all, who is above all, and through all, and in you all."

To put what Paul is saying in verses 1-6 in a short summary, he is being someone who belongs to God, he is pleading for us to fulfill our calling rightly, and in the meantime staying humble, and loving all those around us, both friends and enemies, and all the while keeping our personal relationship with God intact. Doing this allows God to be one with us and this is what He hopes for. Let's continue in Ephesians 4:7-16,

"But unto every one of us is given grace according to the measure of the Gift of Christ. Wherefore he saith, When he ascended up on high, he led captivity captive and gave gifts unto men. (Now that he ascended, what is it but that he also descended first into the lower parts of the earth? He who descended, is the same who ascended up into heaven, to glorify him who reigneth over all heavens, that he might fill all things.)"

Again the word shows He is in and through all things.
"And he gave some, apostles; and some, prophets; and some,

evangelists; and some, pastors and teachers; For the perfecting of the saints, for the work of the ministry, for the edifying of the body of Christ."

It's clear that God works here individually with each of us, and He gives gifts that we use with our neighbors so that they can be edified by our gifts as we are with them. Thus collectively we are strengthening the body of Christ.

"Till we, in the unity of the faith, all come to the knowledge of the Son of God, unto a perfect man, unto the measure of the stature of the fullness of Christ; That we henceforth be no more children, tossed to and fro, and carried about with every wind of doctrine, by the sleight of men, and cunning craftiness, whereby they lie in wait to deceive;"

Here it is said that by individually strengthening our relationship with God, we in turn edify the body of Christ, and this action helps us to see those who are out to deceive us or prolong our advancement in the Christian faith. That is why, at the beginning of this book in my introduction, I pray to God that if any of this information is at fault, that the Lord will show you and you won't be deceived. And that is the way it should be with all that we hear or read. Take it to God in our quest to seek him in all things so we can be assured.

"But speaking the truth in love, may grow up into him in all things, which is the head, even Christ; From whom the whole body fitly joined together and compacted by that which every joint supplieth, according to the effectual working the measure of every part, maketh increase of the body unto the edifying of itself in love."

Reiterating the fact that each of us is a member of the body of Christ, and collectively we share in the strengthening by our actively loving one another. "...fitly joined together" we become like a puzzle each one of us a single piece that creates the body of Christ, the Church. To summarize verses 12-16, I believe Paul is saying that to enlighten His church to a point of the fullness of Christ, and not be swayed in confusion, we must first begin to speak truths in a loving manner, and this is connecting us closer to God, and He will then begin to reveal more of Himself to us. Our continued efforts of focus on Love in this manner will strengthen our relationship with Him, and this edifies the body of Christ. This process of allowing is our agency working with His

Law to do His will, and this process equals God's government.

An example of this "Love" we need to share with others happened when I was living in Germany with my wife and, then, only daughter, Tasha. Tasha was only three or four years old and Maria and I told her it would not be a very big Christmas when it came to presents because we did not have a lot of money. At her age, we felt she understood pretty well. Maria always liked to have boxes to put presents in, so they would look nicer. She found a cracker box just the right size to put a pretty sweater in that she had bought for Tasha. Christmas morning when Tasha saw the presents she became very excited and was smiling from ear to ear. The first box she opened was the present wrapped in the cracker box. When she ripped off the paper she saw that it was a box of crackers, her smile went to almost a frown. Then, as quickly as she changed her expression, we could tell she realized that her parents were still watching her, and instantly, before ever looking up to us, she returned her smile and wide-eyed look. She then looked at us and said, "Thank you so much! You bought me crackers! My favorite." (Now take a minute and picture this episode.) Holding back her tears of joy Maria said, "No, No,

Honey, there is something else in the box!" Tasha regained the genuine look of excitement and found the beautiful sweater inside.

    I tell this story to show the allowance children sometimes make for God to work through them. More than her own, Tasha was concerned with what her parents were feeling. Many times adults, every very devoted adults, have a hard time with this. Jesus was the ultimate example for us. He knew the law of Moses, and He knew the scriptures like many in His time, but He also knew God's love, and those who followed Him learned a lot when Jesus went to dine with the tax collector. The very devoted disciples began to point fingers and tear down the tax collector. They failed to see the reason Jesus wanted to go in that den of sin, not to participate in the sin, but to take His example among the sinners, to tell the parable of the protocol son. That fell on the ears of everyone who was there and it brought Peter and Mathew together.

    A story I heard on the radio, and I do not have all the details, but I do have the most important parts. There was a husband and wife who were having troubles, not only in their marriage but with life in general. The wife never really got along with her mother-in-law, so they rarely talked. One day, the wife decided to swallow her pride and call the mother-in-law for advice. She asked her what she did for her son when he felt bad as a child. The mother-in-law said she remembered that he always liked creamed peas, and when he felt bad, she would always fix them and they would make him feel better. The wife thanked her mother-in-law, and that night when her husband got home after another rough day at work, he saw the creamed peas on the table with his wife standing close by with a smile.

This story again shows where she was thinking more of the feelings of another over those of herself, and all in the name of love, (God). Today so many of us know the scriptures when we hear them or listen to sermons containing the gospel. Yet we still struggle with the tearing down of others, gossiping, and comparing, because we focus on the wrongs of others instead of repenting of our wrongs and loving those we disagree with. A lot of times we don't confront the ones we are upset with, but instead gossip and hold it in behind their backs, and if we do confront them, it is in a disrespectful way and a condemning attitude. Or, if we are approached, we take offense, no matter how polite the person doing the approaching. And worst of all there are the times when we either don't see we are wrong in the first place, or we don't want to admit it.

All of this because we follow what society has sanctioned. We follow our individual lust, and we have grown sheep-minded and too timid to fight against the world. Let's continue and read verses 17-19 in Ephesians.

"This I say therefore, and testify in the Lord, that ye henceforth walk not as other Gentiles walk, in the vanity of their mind, having the understanding darkened, being alienated from the life of God through the ignorance that is in them, because of the blindness of their heart; Who being past feeling have given themselves over unto lasciviousness, to work all uncleanness with greediness."

In this area of Paul's writing, I believe the message is to use our agency and not accept all of the world's teachings. We do this with a discerning heart, and not just hear or read the Word, but also practice it. If not we will not grow closer to Him and at our judgment He will say, "I never knew you" because our hearts have waxed cold. Ephesians 4:20-24 says we must do this, put off the old and put on the new. And we do this by using our agency to allow God, who is Love, to work through our hearts and by understanding His Love and acting accordingly with Him. Then in verse 25 it says, "**wherefore putting away lying, speak every man truth with his neighbor; for we are members one of another.**"

Members? How? Through His true Church which is alive. His Church is the relationship we choose to have with His love, which is mysterious, beautiful, and spiritual. And if I do it, and you do it with Him, that makes you and I members because we become connected to each other through God, through Love. We must grasp this truth. Finally versed 26-32,

"**Can ye be angry, and not sin? Let not the sun go down upon your wrath; Neither give place to the devil. let him that stole steal no more; but rather let him labor, working with his hands for thethings which are good, that he may have to give to him that needeth. Let no corrupt communication proceed out of your mouth, but that which is good to the use of edifying, that it may minister grace unto the hearers. And grieve not the Holy Spirit of God, whereby ye are sealed unto the day of redemption. Let all bitterness, and wrath, and anger, and clamor, and evil speaking, be put away from you, with all malice; and be ye kind one to another, tenderhearted, forgiving one another, even as God for Christ's sake hath forgiven you."

    Brothers and Sisters, I am but a struggling Christian, as many of us are. I know how hard it is to do God's will. But let me tell you--it's not God's will that is hard. It's our agencies' attachment to the ways of the world, society's strong hold of contentment, sheep-minded attitudes, and temptations of the flesh that binds our efforts. I was asked once, "What is the strength to conquer those obstacles, Gregg? Where can I find that Hidden motivation to physically do those things God wants me to?. How can I receive peace and prosperity and oneness with His Church?" It is not a riddle, my Beloved, but an understanding, an understanding of His grace for us. His Love for us. And letting His Love and Grace always work with our actions toward others. We do this along with our repentance, our baptism and confirmation, and we will be counted among His Church.

    Search the scriptures. Study them, pray often, fast and

then practice what God shows us to be true. Then use this knowledge to *"Live God's Church."*

"People are often unreasonable, illogical, and self-centered; Forgive them anyway. If you are kind, people may accuse you of selfish, ulterior motives; Be kind anyway. If you are successful you will win some false friends and true enemies; Succeed anyway. If you are honest and frank, people may cheat you; Be honest and frank anyway. What you spend years building, someone could destroy overnight; Build anyway. If you find serenity and happiness, they may be jealous; Be happy anyway. The good you do today, people will often forget tomorrow, Do good anyway. Give the world the best you have, and it may never be enough; Give the world the best you've got anyway. You see, in the final analysis, it is between you and God; it was never between you and them anyway."

~Mother Teresa

Chapter Five
Finding Your Way

So far in this book there has been a common focus. This focus is from Mark chapter 12, and I believe this is the most important for our walk with Christ. To love God with all our souls, hearts, minds, and strength and to love our neighbors and ourselves equally. Jesus said there is no other commandment greater than these. None. But how many of us hear this word of God and ponder upon it? How many of us go to the Lord in prayer for real understanding? I am here now telling you this is a message of God and it still is here today. It is not a message from Gregg or a denomination, but from God, and it is throughout scripture.

This chapter is designed for, what I believe is something to get us to listen to what God's message is to all of us. If you remember the chapter on the four tools and the significance of them, you'll remember the soul needs to be filled with the Spirit of God or the Holy Ghost. The level to which it is filled is the level to which our mind, or agency, has allowed it to be filled. This is the decisions we make as individuals and when we choose to hear, read and study the Word of God, and take those understandings which He gives us, and live His Church we increase our chances of being filled completely, even to the fullness of Christ. But again, how many of us really do this, or how many of us just hear and become sheep-minded and go the easy route? The route with little effort.

In Mosiah 8:21 we read, **"All we like sheep have gone astray; We have turned, everyone, to his own way; And the Lord hath laid on Him the iniquities of us all."** How do good people, who want to do the right thing go astray? It would be easy to say that the devil made them do it, but, in fact, it is the good people's agency that causes them to be content with being sheep minded. Now the Lord calls us His sheep, and He is our Shepard, but does He want us to be sheep-minded? I say to you, "No."

I like to tell a story at camps of a young Indian boy and a coyote. I first heard it from a man named Bill Miller a Native Indian song writer. It goes like this;

There was once a little Native American boy who loved

the sound of the whip-poor-will. So one night he set out looking for him so he could watch him sing. The land was rough to travel and it wasn't easy for the young boy to reach his goal. Suddenly he came upon a well-worn path that made his travel much easier. He stayed on it until he came upon a coyote.

"Why are you following me, boy?" said the coyote. "I'm not, Mr. Coyote, I am trying to get to where the whip-poor-will sings so I can watch him and your path as made it easy for me to follow the singing of the whip-poor-will." said the boy

Then the coyote asked; "Don't you like my songs?" The boy said yes but he added that he preferred the sound of the whip-poor-will. The coyote told the boy to listen to his night song and the coyote reared back his head and yodeled out a tune. When the coyote was done, the boy slowly brought his hands down from his ears and said; "Thank you for the song, Mr. Coyote, but I much prefer the song of the whip-poor-will."

This made the coyote furious so he told the boy that he knew a short cut to where the whip-poor-will sang, as the coyote smiled out of the side of his mouth, and, with an outstretched paw, points in a certain direction. The boy, realizing that it was getting late, agreed to follow the coyote. The coyote took off over the rough layout of the land with a mild gallop while the boy struggled to keep up. Eventually the boy fell, and the coyote stopped and told the boy to hurry up and that they were almost there.

Again the boy followed and again he fell, this time in a gopher hole where he twisted his knee. By this time the boy realized it was morning and the song of the whip-poor-will had stopped. In fact, the boy could hear the cries of the coyote in a distant field. The boy limped home covered in burs, mosquito bites, cuts and bruises and a banged up knee.

It wasn't until many summers later when the boy became an older and much wiser man that he realized that in life there are many paths to reach goals, and the easiest ones to travel are not always the best ones to take. Most of all, in our quest to reach ultimate happiness, we must always be on the lookout for coyote.

Our adversary is the coyote, the devil. The devil knows that we sit complacent as sheep as we come to our denominations half filled with the Spirit to wait for that mountain top experience and a tunnel of light to guide us to salvation or the Promised

Land. This is exactly what the devil wants us to think. He doesn't want us to figure out that to come to the fullness of Christ we must do so by the Love of God, Mark pointed this out. We must read, study, pray, and fast according to that which we hear in God's Word. So the devil doesn't want us to study and take this message of God, in fact, he probably would prefer for us to just say, "That was a good message" and then put the book down and forget about it and never actually ponder on the message at all.

He doesn't want us to agree that we must work within ourselves acts of kindness, sel<u>fless</u>ness, non-comparability with others, or to always love others or to speak out loud to defend this way of life and attitude.

Scripture tells us that the adversary is the lord of this world. Why? Because society is the coyote trying to make us believe the right way is the easy way, not stand up for what we know is right and not to rock the boat. We are to know that if we are lead by the shepard of evil that it's not so bad and if we just live life the best we can and enjoy the "feel good" things, as long as they are not hurting anyone else, then that is okay. We just have to believe, and this makes us content sheep feeling we are doing that which is right. I remember when I lived in Germany in 1987 that here in the United States there was a rash of flag burners, and a lot of debate came from it. Many people felt it was freedom of speech and that it was no big deal to burn a rag, to burn a piece of cloth that represented "one nation under God." They said that it was a freedom of expression, so many people, like sheep, didn't say anything. Didn't do anything. Didn't fight. They disagreed but mostly on just an internal basis. Because of that, there are states now that give people the right to express themselves in this manner.

Let's talk about our voting practices, those who even take the time to vote, that is. So many people vote for the party they belong to, sheepishly following the directions of their party without really researching where they are heading, who is on the ticket or what they really stand for. The majority do not vote for the person they believe is right for our nation but just for the party they are representing. The party they belong to should not matter. My father always told me not to mix politics and religion, but I cannot separate the two, nor do I feel our founding fathers meant for us to separate them. Separation of church and state was only formed so that the Government could not tell us how and where we could worship and how to live the "church." But now we have the likes of the ACLU that are becoming a tool of tyranny over our Christian heritage and our rights of expression. People become uncomfortable with those who rock the boat. Would we be comfortable with Moses, John the Baptist, or Jesus, all of whom rocked the boat by standing up for what they knew was right. I tell you it seems to me that the ACLU would have all of them put in jail if they could. We need to remember the leaders of this organization in our prayers that they might see the terrible eroding they are causing of this blessed nation.

With our pledge of allegiance, to state "one nation under God" is unconstitutional in the some states. Coyote feels it is wrong to have our children acknowledge God in the pledge, so many are sheep-minded and, as long as it is not hurting them, they do not fight it. We must take the first step. Once we do, then our Lord Jesus will guide us the rest of the way because we made that choice.

We must pray, fast, and act on others with the Love of God. Do this individually and collectively and God will be our

Shepard. He will guide us. In the Book of Mormon there is a vision of the rod of iron. We are to hold fast to it until we reach everlasting life. The rod of iron is the Word of God. The word of God is the fuel that gives us strength.

Show me a sheep that has been complacent for a long time, and I'll show you an animal that is cowardly. Some of us are like this, and are constantly letting things go, and saying to ourselves "I am okay, so why bother?" Or we stay interested in ourselves as long as we do not hurt anyone else or we walk away from those things we disagree with, only to let someone else deal with them. When we do this for a long time, and then something happens to us, where we do not have a choice but to act, we become afraid to say anything because we do not want people to dislike us or say anything behind our backs. Sheep-minded is not always good.

I am not a doomsday person, but I do believe we are in the last days, and I do believe the scriptures when they talk of the horrible things yet to take place, such as the number of the beast and not being able to buy food or other things without it. Those who believe in Christ will be outlaws. I can see the writing on the wall and if we keep our sheep-minded attitudes, we will fall into the hands of the world and not be counted among His people. We cannot say, "When that time comes I'll be different." Because then it will be too late, and we will already have been deceived in following the shepard of evil too far into the wilderness.

Again, we have an opportunity to do God's intended work. Trust in Jesus and His guidance with your heart and love others as Jesus instructed. We need to prepare ourselves, for He already prepared the way for our agency to work.

If I could be just a fraction of what Jesus was in His compassion, and love for us, I would be a far better person than I am today. I hope to God that when I put this book down that I will go to God in prayer and study so that I too can be filled with His Spirit and that I can continue to ask Him to help me make the right decisions in order to do His work.

Today my youngest daughter, Alora, talked to me about her training for the coming track season. In short, we talked about how far does she need to push herself in practice so that she can do well in the actual race. I told her that it is the same as when

I was training soldiers in the Army. We really do need to train as we will fight. They cannot say, "This is only training and when the action really comes we will be different." That kind of mentality has killed a lot of soldiers and has lost a lot of races. To do good in our race we must overcome our weaknesses with the preparation prior to the race. If we wait until the race to do so, to put all out, then it is too late.

It is the same in our Christian walk. If we wait for that mountain top experience or the heavens to open before we begin to prepare ourselves, it will be too late. I know it becomes hard to see what lies along our way. We have obstacles that, if not negotiated, we will fail. It is hard to see those obstacles; so sometimes we want to see the un-seeable by using analogies of things we can see to explain the mysterious, yet wonderful, way God created us, and what He wants us to do. Let's try to understand the route we must choose to find our way in this world, to find the path that He wants us to walk.

First we must understand our obstacles and that which stands in our way. When I was in the Army, I was pretty handy in land navigation. In fact, as a Ranger, that was on e of the primary skills we needed to be proficient in. We would receive an operations order and a map from our superiors. They would show us on the map where we were and where we needed to go. They would also explain why we had to be at point B, why it was important and the circumstances of our mission. We would listen to him and understand the mission, but it didn't stop there because we would actually have to go from point A to point B. We didn't just hear about the mission. We didn't just understand why we had to go. We would physically have to live our movements from point A to B, and everything in-between. Along the way we would meet obstacles that stood in our way. And guess what would create those obstacles. Each individual situation determines what type of obstacles would be in our way and many times we never knew until we were there. Those situations would cause us to make a choice of routes, whether to go through, over, under or around. Then to negotiate the obstacle we first, had to come to an understanding of them because if we didn't, we were not going to be able to accomplish our mission. If we just looked on the map and saw swamps, deserts and mountains and just said "Okay, we just have to swim the swamps, cross the desert and climb the mountains," we might understand it, but it is a lot harder to physically accomplish it once we get in that situation. We find ourselves asking if we were really prepared to tackle this mission and these obstacles.

Guess how we came to an understanding of each type of obstacle. We practiced, and researched, all possible obstacles during our training prior to coming into a situation that called for our actual negotiations of it. We spend hundreds of hours reading, asking, preparing, and practicing our swamp, desert, and mountain survival techniques. It's the same in sports, business, and life. In our Christian walk and understandings we tend to just hear the instruction or preaching, and see point A and point B on our map of Christian life, and even go as far as to understand why, but if we do not practice and research that information with God before we find ourselves in these situations, we will fail.

I remember when I was a little boy, my dad would put out rules that we must follow, so we would learn and not get into trouble. He would say things like; "Boys, make sure you stay away from my tools in the garage because you might get hurt. If you do, you will get into trouble." We heard him, and we understood what he was saying and didn't want to get hurt or into trouble, that was for sure. Two or three days later we would be playing outside, and next thing we knew, we would find ourselves next to the tools in the garage. Just three days earlier we had heard dad and understood why he had these rules, but we were playing, having fun, and were not being scolded or taught something by him. We were not thinking about things, but just living life as we went. We then began playing with the tools. The situation did not sink in, but why didn't it? Because we did not practice and research the situation enough for it to be in our minds. Now us being children at the time maybe is saying that it is more of the parents job to give us examples and teach more but the outcome is the same. God however did give us an example by giving us Jesus Christ and He does continue to teach us in the scriptures.

Going back to the obstacles, how do we understand them? Again, we practice and research. When we go out, every single situation is different and can bring many different obstacles, no matter how small or large the situation is. We have to practice what we know of the Word of God. Because of practice and research, we become more capable of understanding what we need to do to negotiate each obstacle we come to. We practice every single day of our lives. We practice the Word of God in every aspect of our lives, with our children, spouses, brothers, sisters, parents; in our work place with bosses, employees, friends, etc.

It is the obstacles that we do not understand that bog us down and prevents us from accomplishing our mission. And guess what the number one obstacle out there is. The obstacle that is the foundation to all other obstacles. That obstacle is the one of SELF. Self Love is the tool that the coyote loves to use the most. However, didn't the Word say to love others as we do ourselves? Yes, but we are not supposed to love ourselves more than we do our neighbors. In other words, we are to love others, to sacrifice, to put the well being of others before ourselves as Christ does in the Church. We are not to compare our well being to that of theirs or take care of ourselves first. Life is not a score card. The idea is that we develop a relationship that we have with God which engulfs every single contact that we make. In every single contact we have with others, we should share, show and allow our relationship with God to be in control, and that contact is the practice we use from our research of His Word. That practice becomes our strength because it lives within us. He lives within us and all those we come in contact with will benefit from our actions. The only self God wants us to understand is the relationship we ourselves have with others. There is a difference in these two selves. It's very important that the love we feel in our relationships shines through in every situation, even with those who hate us or whom we disagree with. We are loving all as Christ does the church. To fail and to not negotiate the obstacle of self is to put our self-gratification above all else. That very act of selfishness is of the devil. We then begin to compare and critique others shortcomings to make ourselves feel better. This then becomes a spiritual cancer that builds inside us and becomes one of those obstacles that halts our personal growth and salvation.

    This is the key. God's love, which we have in us, is not the me first mentality. It is the love relationship where He lives in and through all things as we interact with the world. In Ephesians 3:8-21,

    "Unto me, who am less than the least of all saints, is this

grace given, that I should preach among the Gentiles the unsearchable riches of Christ; And to make all men see what is the fellowship of the mystery, which from the beginning of the world hath been hid in God, who created all things by Jesus Christ; To the intent that now unto the principalities and powers in heavenly places might be known by the church the manifold wisdom of God. According to the eternal purpose which he purposed in Christ Jesus our Lord; In whom we have boldness and access with confidence by the faith of him. Wherefore I desire that ye faint not at my tribulations for you, which is your glory. For this cause I bow my knees unto the Father of our Lord Jesus Christ, of whom the whole family in heaven and earth is named, that He would grant you, according to the riches of His glory, to be strengthened with might by His Spirit in the inner man; That Christ may swell in your hearts by faith; that ye, being rooted and grounded in love, may be able to comprehend with all saints what is the breadth, and length, and depth, and height; And to know the love of Christ, which passeth knowledge, that ye might be filled with all the fullness of God. Now unto Him that is able to do exceeding abundantly above all that we ask or thing, according to the power that worketh in us, Unto Him be glory in the church by Christ Jesus throughout all ages, world without end. Amen."

 Self does become a horrid obstacle if we cannot live the church as the Word of God asked us to. Our self-gratification is standing above that which God is wanting us to live by, because we are too prideful to let go of this obstacle. Paraphrasing something Gandhi said about Christians, he said that if Christians lived only half of what Christianity teaches, there would be far more peace in the world. And this is true. It is too easy to hold on to our self-obstacle and our society today condones that very way of life.

 We search the world for answers on how to get to point B, and because we do not practice and research we end up taking the easy path, the one that coyote has set for us. We then become lost and depressed because we cannot find our way there. All this does is turn us toward our comforting self gratification and leads us to an even deeper disappointment; and the adversary wins again, because we are choosing the easy route, the route that makes us feel a part of society, and this somehow, in turn, makes us feel we have more authority.

From Galatians 6:8, **"For he that soweth to his flesh shall of the flesh reap corruption."** Self-gratification leads to what? The Word says corruption. This is where we become of the world and not just in the world. We become lost even though we know why we want to get to point B. We want to feel good, happy and instead we have to deal with disappointments, depressions, and sadness. **"But he that soweth to the Spirit shall of the Spirit reap life everlasting."** That is, that peace, that love, that tranquility, that we keep searching for. That is the point B we are trying to reach.

By now we understand the greatest commandments that we find in Mark chapter 12 To love God with our soul, heart, mind and strength. <u>This commandment is exactly the same relationship mentality that this book is speaking of, the same relationship that has God living within us, and the love that we practice with when we interact in the world. This relationship equals our active life, is loving our neighbors as we do ourselves and is using our heart, soul, mind and strength, to love God with.</u> All of that is negotiating the obstacle of self. We must learn to get rid of satisfying me, myself and I. We must do this with our individual research of His Word so that we might learn to be more sel<u>less</u>.

In today's society our media is continually pumping the "me first mentality", the self-gratification <u>feel good first</u> mentality, and our culture is changing for the worst because of this. If we take the hunt out of the lion and keep it in a cage, what happens? It becomes lonely, depressed, weak, and overtime, eventually loses its way of life and ultimately its' life. The same is true of our nation. It was founded on Christian principles and doctrine, and no matter how anyone tries to spin it, we cannot take that fact away. And as soon as society takes those values and doctrine out of our government, we will grow more greedy, depressed, weak and ultimately lose that which gave us our greatness; **"One Nation Under God."** What we think, what we practice and research is what we will become. That is very important. Our fate, everyone's fate, is in our choices, and in our agency. How we choose to get to point B in our lives, has everything to do with our relationship with God, no matter how small it is. And our relationship with God has everything to do with our politics, and government. This all begins with us as individuals. All actions should be done in the Name of God. Keep Him as our rod of iron as we live our lives. By doing this we begin to negotiate that which bogs us down, self gratification. We begin to find our way and make it to point B.

"America is like a healthy body and it's resistance is threefold: its patriotism, its morality, and its spiritual life. If we can undermine these three areas, America will collapse from within."

~Josef Stalin

Chapter Six
The Kingdom of God vs. the Great Abominable Church

What is the Kingdom of God? Why is it so hard to figure out what God wants us to understand? For centuries these questions have plagued mankind, even to a point that different interpretations of the Word of God have caused more separation and conflict than the peace and unity we have all been seeking in the first place. As I am writing this chapter, a war is going on in the Middle East; a war between my country, the United States of America, and Iraq. Saddam Hussein, the president of Iraq, is a very evil dictator who suppresses his people with fear, torture, and even death. Yet our society in America is quickly becoming more twisted in its purposes within our government and around the world, and it is hard for a lot of people to completely trust the intentions of our government. I feel this is a just war and hope that my government is fighting for the moral purpose to free the Iraqi people and not for some hidden purposes.

But what does this war have to do with the above questions? I brought it up to show, at this time in history, all of the twisted things that surround this war. We have Saddam stating that God will provide for them, that God is on his side and he attempts to somehow lead us to believe that God condones torturing men, women and children to satisfy his greed as a dictator. Then our president believes God is on his side because our foundation is "One nation under God," but as his speech's might gain the support of the American citizens when focused on the war, these very same citizens are battling in our courts about whether we should keep the country as a nation under God. The Ten Commandments are being banned from our courtrooms and it is proposed the pledge of allegiance phrase "under God" be stricken from the pledge. Separation of Church and State is becoming a governmental control of our citizens' worship, and our constitutional right in our public arenas are slowly decaying. I believe with all my heart that this nation was indeed a gift to mankind. Millions of people have fought and died for the very Christian principles that our nation was founded upon. This country is truly a God given gift to the people of the world, through inspiration, revelation, prayer and obedience to His law; but it is also true to say we are slowly but surely losing that gift. The inspiration that early American received to help develop this country were of God. But like many times throughout history, the minute God gives man a gift, the adversary is not far behind to try and divert its purpose. Now this is very important to say here. The devil cannot mess with the gift of God itself, but what he can mess with is our interpretation of that gift. He attacks us to try and disgrace God through tiny twists and tweaks our interpretations. He does this through justifying sel_fish_ feelings and molding what feels good to us with that which is God's law. Then, if that wasn't bad enough, because of this manipulation by the devil, denominations of all kinds are fighting against one another while proclaiming their religion is the right one and all others are wrong, even within Christian denominations.

    I have a picture I clipped from a newspaper during the first Gulf War in 1991, that shows a typical satan rendition with the horns, tail and long finger nails, laying on his side cocked up on one elbow, while his other hand is playing with tiny humans that are at war with one another. On each human they have written on them what their religious affiliation is; Catholic, Jew, Moslem, Christian, etc. Of course the humans are mad, killing one another and dying while satan has a big smile on his face. The caption under the picture is two words in quotations, "One God." This is quite scary, but in today's society it is true. The adversary, through time, has systematically lead good people, as well as the bad, to this state of deception. From Adam till now, satan has been deceiving the world a fraction at a time. For generation after generation our minds have become clouded through his manipulation of the truth and then his using man to disgrace God. The kicker is that we actually believe we are doing what is right most of the time and we are totally unaware of the damage we are causing ourselves and those around us. The caption on that newspaper cartoon is true to the extent of those people's perception, but it leaves out the ultimate truth. That is that the "one God" is the same God who created us, the same God who sent His only begotten Son in Jesus the Christ to die for our sins. But there is more to the ultimate truth. There are but two masters in this world, one of greater power than the other, but two masters none the less. God and satan. These two masters are not equal due to God being the one who created the devil, but both are the heads of two followings, the church of the world and the true church of God. What is the true kingdom of God? What church is the right church to show us the kingdom? For centuries this question has plagued mankind, and for centuries the doors were opened to those who were seeking Him, and yet we still fall short of that glory.

Now that I have beat this horse to death, lets see what the Word says about the Kingdom of God. The book of Matthew shows many parables that teach the Kingdom of Heaven and Jesus says He must teach in parables because those who do not come to know God on their own accord will not understand; but those who do, do come to an understanding.

Chapter 13:9-13 in the Inspired Version contains the parable of the sower and this is the first one we will examine, 13:3-4, **"And he spake many things unto them in parables, saying, Behold, a sower went forth to sow. And when he sowed some seeds fell by the wayside, and the fowls came and devoured them up."** Now in verse 18 Jesus gives the meaning, saying; **"When any one heareth the word of the kingdom, and** understandeth not, then cometh the wicked one, and catcheth away that which was sown in his heart; this is he who received seed by the wayside." This is clear. It's true with the word of God and His teachings; if we do not experience it, if we do not get into it, and not just hear the Word preached, but study and ponder it within our hearts to get the spiritual witness, that affects our spiritual being; then, I tell you, you do not understand. That is what opens the door for the devil to come into our hearts, which is our tool of discernment, and takes away our acceptance of the fullness. Thus we are falling by the wayside. A lot of us do not want to admit that we might have this type of shallow Christianity. We cannot just go though the motions without truly developing a covenant relationship with our Lord Jesus Christ. By that I mean if we do not make a covenant with Him by truly repenting of our ways and truly believe that we are going to be obedient in changing our old selves into our new selves by developing a covenant relationship with our Lord, we will fall by the way side. We must experience this personal relationship with God.

He continues in verse 5; **"Some fell upon stony places, where they had not much earth; and forth with they sprung up;**

and when the sun was up, they were scorched, because they had no deepness of earth; and because they had no root, they withered away." And in verse 19 Jesus explains;

"But he that received the seed into stony places, the same is he that heareth the word and readily with joy receiveth it, yet hath not root in

himself, and endureth but for a while; for when tribulation or persecution ariseth because of the word, by and by he is offended."

This is where most believers are today. We go to our congregations and hear the Word preached, and are joyful because of it, but because we do not study the Word afterward or practice what we hear, when dilemmas or persecutions arise because of the Word, we become offended. This offense is from ignorance, and the ignorance is from the lack of praying, fasting and studying the Word on a personal level. Verse 6; **"And some fell among thorns and thorns sprung up and choked them."** Jesus then explains in verse 20; **"He also who received seed among the thorns, is he that heareth the word; and the care of this world and deceitfulness of riches, choke the word, and he becometh** unfruitful." In other words, this is those of us who feel our possessions and worldly busy life becomes a higher priority to us than pondering on the Word of God that we hear. Because of that, we do not answer our calling from God. But then in verse 7 He says; **"But others fell into good ground, and brought forth fruit; some a hundredfold, some sixty fold and some thirty fold. Who hath ears to hear, let him hear."** In verse 21 He continues; **"But he that received seed into the good ground, is he that heareth the word and understandeth and endureth; which also beareth fruit, and bringeth forth some hundredfold, some sixty and some thirty."** Here is simply those who hear the Word and they do understand it because of their study and practice of the Word and because of this they endure.

This parable is basically telling us that part of the Kingdom of Heaven is, in fact, hearing the Word and then taking that information and putting it to practice. How? By study, prayer and fasting. This is very foundational and very important in being a part of His Kingdom.

Then another parable in Mathew 13:22-29,

"Another parable put he forth unto them, saying the

kingdom of heaven is likened unto a man who sowed good seed in his field; But while he slept, his enemy came and sowed tares among the wheat, and went his way. But when the blade sprung up and brought forth fruit, then appeared the tares also. So the servants of the householder came and said unto him, Sir, didst not thou sow good seed in thy field? When then hath it tares? He said unto them, an enemy hath done this. And the servants said unto him. Wilt thou then that we go and gather them up? But he said, Nay; lest while ye gather up the tares, ye root up also the wheat with them. Let both grow together until the harvest and in the time of harvest, I will say to the reapers, Gather ye together first the wheat in my barn; and the tares are bound in bundles to be burned."

    Jesus tells the disciples the meaning of this parable in verses 36-44. He said the field is the world, the good seed is the children of the kingdom, the tares are the children of the wicked, the enemy is the devil, the harvest is the end of the world or the destruction of the wicked and the reapers are the angels sent from heaven. He says before His coming the angels will be sent to gather, and then it when the righteous will shine in the kingdom.

This parable explains that another part of the Kingdom of Heaven is living among the wicked until the day that we are to be separated from them. We must think about what the wheat is doing while the tares share in all of our surroundings. This is also very important in understanding His Kingdom.

Another parable is Mathew 13 in verses 30-31;

"And another parable put he forth unto them, saying, the kingdom of heaven is like to a grain of mustard seed, which a man took and sowed in his field; Which indeed is the least of all seeds, but when grown, it is the greatest among herbs, and becometh a tree, so that the birds of the air come and lodge in the branches thereof."

This one is not specifically broke down for the disciples, but taking the same definitions with the field being the world, God is saying the very least of His seeds, His children, can not only grow to be the greatest of all the seeds, but also give refuge to those in need and not like themselves. This parable points out yet another part of the Kingdom of Heaven, which is being the least by the world's standards, but to trust in God's handling of us so when we grow within His Kingdom, we will do great work for the

Kingdom. This trust and growth is essential for the good works to take place.

Another parable in Mathew 13 is in verse 32, **"Another parable spake he unto them, the Kingdom of Heaven is like unto leaven, which a women took and hid in three measures of meal, till the whole was leavened."** This one is short and sweet. Leaven is a substance that causes fermentation and, when put with meal, over time the process continues until all is fermented. Webster says fermentation is the decomposition of organic substances produced by the action of a living organism. I believe this parable points out an important activity of the kingdom of heaven is by the Father, the Son, and the Holy Spirit, as they work in us to decompose wickedness, and as we continue to accept God's plan of action we rise into that which feeds others. And another, verse 46, **"And again, the kingdom of heaven is like unto a treasure hid in a field. And when a man hath found a treasure which is hid, he secureth it, and , straightway, for joy thereof, goeth and selleth all that he hath, and buyeth that field."** This one is a little tougher. The understanding is the kingdom is the treasure, and the field is the world. It seems to me that we find the treasures of the kingdom hidden in the world, and in turn we are joyful and do away with all worldly things in order to buy the world in the new spiritual treasure of heaven, which is understanding.

Another factor of the kingdom of heaven is understanding God's kingdom, which brings happiness and, in turn we no longer have interests in worldly cares, but more important is sharing our new understanding so that others in the world will also be blessed. This makes us rich in spiritual treasures.

Now all of these parables tell us what the kingdom of God is like. When we put the meanings of all these from Mathew together, I think we get a pretty good picture of what the kingdom of God is like it will be here on earth.

The kingdom of God for us is like this. We are in the field, society, planted by God. Within the world there is a hidden understanding of the meaning of life and God's plan for us. We must prepare for finding this understanding by hearing the Word of God and then studying it, praying about its contents and fasting for insight. After this we must practice in life that which we have nurtured by understanding and even though we are surrounded by wicked and lost people, in the end, we have the assurance that we will be separated from the evil. We must not get caught up in the covetness and pride which the world wants us to have, but we must become meek and the least of the world's cares by serving others and spreading the good news of the treasure found. This will produce good works here on earth and further God's plan of establishing His Church. When we do this, we aid in God's work which will eventually separates all evil and the righteous will rise.

We read in scripture that there are but two churches, God's and the devil's. So we must not confuse man-governed denominations as true churches of God, but account them for what they are, man-governed places of fellowship. Places where like-minded people come and worship God as a group, or better put, they are remnants of the true body of Christ. It is the remnant believers that are the Church, not the denomination they affiliate themselves with. This one understanding alone has caused so much strife in the world. But we cannot, must not, allow the adversary to put ides of self-pride over that which God has set. His order and His rule, over His creation.

Webster's dictionary defines the word abominable as "to detest extremely" or "to loathe." The word church is defined as "a building for Christian worship" and " a denomination of the Christian religion." Even here the church is given as a man created place, so it still misses the essential power of the Being. More on that topic later. To combine the two, Webster says that the great abominable church is a great building of Christian worship that is loathful. Or, shorter put, "A loathful worshiping Christian building." We know that a building cannot worship nor loathe. Thus creating the very problem of the world's definition of a church. So we know it must be the members of all congregations that are collectively joined together by principalities and tweaked beliefs that make up this loathful church. I hope you can follow along with this message. I belong to the restoration remnant or denomination, not because I want to restore the Reorganized Church of the Latter Day Saints church. I belong to the restoration movement because I believe we are now in the absolute prime position to restore the true Church of God. Because we have not been totally deceived nor gone astray of what God's Word teaches. We try our best to have a backbone in this society we live in today and tell them "No." It's not okay to be gay. It's not okay to change the role of men and women from what the Bible teaches. "Wives submit to their husbands" does not mean for them to do what they are told but to abide in him spiritually, and for "husbands to love your wives as Christ did the Church," with love and compassion, understanding, support, with charity and sel<u>les</u>sness. It's not because we hate women, or gays, or whatever else churches are conforming with society about. It's because the Word of God is unchanging, the same yesterday as it will be tomorrow. We should not just say; "Well, we love everyone," or "We must be tolerant of everyone." and believe this goes for the things they do as well. Hate the sin not the sinner. Again, this is just satan taking something that seems good and tweaking it just a little to deceive us and disgrace God at the same time; and that is the beginnings of the abominable church. There is a movement in the restoration that we as sinners must repent and focus on what God is telling us.

If we look in 1 Nephi 3:140-44, an angel shows Nephi the formation of the great abominable church.

"And the angel said unto me: "Behold the formation of the church which is most abominable above all other churches, Which slayeth the saints of God, yea, and

tortureth them, and bindeth them down, and yoketh them with a yoke of iron, and bringeth them down into captivity." And it comes to pass that I beheld this great and abominable church; and I saw the devil, that he was the founder of it; and I also saw gold and silver and silks and scarlets and fine-twined linen and all manner of precious clothing and the harlots are the desires of this great and abominable church; And also for the praise of the world do they destroy the saints of God and bring them down into captivity."

Now if we look for a denomination that fits this bill we will not be able to leave out any, not one, where its members do not suffer from these types of temptations and hardships. If we look at the individual denomination as an abominable church, then we start becoming prideful and pointing fingers at the Catholics or the Mormons, etc. But look again at the end of this verse, "...the desires of this great and abominable church; and also for the praise of the world do they destroy the saints of God and bring them down into captivity." It is what the adversary does to the saints that destroys them and brings them into captivity. Don't you see? Does that mean this abominable church does not exist?

No. The devil wants us to believe so, but scripture also tells us that this church, the great abominable church, has formed its greatness with the Gentiles. I believe it is here in my country, the United States of America, as well as all over the world wherever there are people. But here in the U.S. I see it as a leader, but why? Because here God blessed a land and its people, and helped to inspire its Government. Because of that, the devil hates America, and again, over a period of time worked the twisting of the inspired truth to deceive mankind for the disgrace of God. That is why we are now battling the right to claim our Creator in any of our public and governmental places, and this is why our media from video games to movies to advertisements are filled with money making, precious clothing, sex and power, all the very fabric that is replacing our society's foundation. This is due to lust and greed as the scripture touched on above, and this is influencing the minds of our children, ourselves, our politicians and the society that votes them in.

So here we see that a part of the great abominable church seems to occur when the children of man seek and desire riches, fine things, and physical lusts, and compartmentalizing a building or a denomination as a church, for satan is making sure we separate the two situations. Satan wants us to go to church and hear the good news without further study or personal pondering outside of where we worship. He wants us to go home after church to a separate environment and continue on with our worldly lives away from the Word of God.

So you see that is satan's purpose in tweaking of the expression "separation of church and state." This is why society is slowly changing our laws to have our government tell us how and where we must worship. Our forefathers would break down and cry if they saw what is now happening with their revelations from God, I have no doubt. The original term was indeed another gift given to us so we would not allow man-governing state to rule over the sovereignty of God. Then satan twisted it to what we are fighting over today.

If we go to 1 Nephi 3:220-223, we read,

"And he saith unto me: "Behold, there are save it be two churches. The one is the church of the Lamb of god, and the other is the church of the devil; Wherefore, whoso belongeth not to the church of the Lamb of God belongeth to that great

church which is the mother of abominations, and she is the whore of all the earth."

Why a whore? Plainly put, a prostitute gives an individual what he or she covets. So the church that is not of God wants to pleasure our wants and the use the "feel good" mentality to justify our participation in it, thus making us a part of this abominable church, even when we think we belong to the right denomination or church building. So again, we are deceived into believing that when we belong to the right church building we are okay.

In the New Testament, Jesus states; **"No man can serve two masters: for either he will hate the one, and love the other; or else he will hold to the one, and despise the other. Ye cannot serve God and mammon."** Mammon means valuable possessions or, again, the riches and desires mentioned above. This "being of the world" is fast becoming common ground and more and more mainstream as these desires grow in popularity. mankind is slowly pushing away God and His sovereignty, and very soon we will be to a point of open worldly "spirituality" that will outlaw Christianity. John 15:19 says, **"If ye were of the world, the world would love his own: but because ye are not of the** world, but I have chosen you out of the world, therefore the world hateth you." We are now well into that process, the process of wanting to be loved by the world, the process that is being fueled by the devil and we are playing those very things out for him for his amusement, and his sovereignty, not God's.

These scriptures tell us that another part of the great and abominable church is actively being separated from the way of life which God wants us participating in, the way of life that His Word teaches us. We do this by our own choice, by choosing the very evil things that are forbidden by God. Indulging in pleasing things become the actual motivating factors to discredit the importance of living a Godly life.

You know, I would like to take a moment here to share something that will shed some more light. I watch a lot of the National Football League, and I am an avid Buffalo Bills fan, to say the least. My interest started during the football season of 1973. My twin brother and I were eight years old, and both of our older brothers had favorite NFL teams. We lived in Nebraska at the time, and there was no local NFL team, so we asked our older brothers how could we get our own favorite team. Our older brothers, Grover and Grady said just wait until Sunday and watch all the games, pick one of the teams and stay with it the rest of your life. So when the weekend came, I was watching one particular very snowy game and I could hardly see the players on the TV. Then it happened. A running back ran a short run, they stopped the game, and the stands gave this man a standing ovation for being the first running back in NFL history to run for 2000+ yards in a single season. His name was O.J. Simpson. I told my brothers that from then on the Buffalo Bills would be my favorite team.

    Through the years I have collected many things from cards, hats, apparel, etc. of the Buffalo Bills. It became fun to have pride in my very own team. When Sundays came around we all would, in fun, tear down the teams of others and defended our own, as if we were actually a part of the team. Each year we looked forward to the season with greater expectations and hopes of our teams greatness and the possible bragging rights we would have over our brothers or friends at school. Soon we would be known as a part of that group we were fans of. When people would see me, and the topic of football might be in the air, they knew I was a Buffalo Bill, the twelfth man on the team, if you will.

I grew older and joined the military and again noticed that I had to choose a brand of service between the Army, Navy, Air force and Marines. This time, when the topic of the military came up, I was identified as a soldier in the Army; but I never stopped my affiliation with the Buffalo Bills, having lots of fun arguing football with my fellow soldiers and service men. Then soon I had the same type of pride when training with the Marines, Seamen, or Airmen. The rivalries between the services became much like the pride we had with the NFL teams, and this pride kept our affiliations strong.

Soon my first presidential vote came into play. For me to vote I had to pick a political party to belong to, I watched and listened to the candidates to see where they stood, weighed each platform with my beliefs, with what was best for my country and chose to vote for Ronald Regan. Now I was a Republican, a soldier, and a Buffalo Bill. All of these are separate, but all were affiliations that were a part of who I am. After all, this was the right thing to do. It was all part of being an American. Right? All of this is very important in my life and seemed necessary in our social functioning and governing within the country.

Then it hit me, it happened right before I started this chapter in November of 2003. How could I not have seen this before? That, yes, even with our denominations, this pride of man-governing stood true. This very same verbalization took place by everyone in our denominations. Catholic vs. Protestants, Jews vs. Christians, Baptists vs. Methodist, Mormons vs. RLDS, etc. We conditioned ourselves from childhood for competitions to be prideful, to dominate, take credit and to belong to the winning side. I began to see it everywhere: my job vs. other jobs, school teams vs. other school teams, communities vs. other communities, we teach our kids in school to take pride in their accomplishments, to pat themselves on the backs. We try to "keep up with the Joneses", neighbor vs. neighbor. When we play board games with friends and family, it's men vs. women, or husbands vs. wives. We begin to point fingers and critique others and their affiliations, a division of a mild yet deceiving level of evil. It is everywhere. Each of the above groups or affiliations are just as important in our lives as the other, it seems. Each is dealt with in the same manner, and has the same foundation that the devil started so many centuries ago by tweaking just slightly, and changing entire cultures into paradigms. It seems to be a self-governing and self-mentality that we all call "life." All the affiliations I spoke of are harmless, that is not my point here. My point is the foundation we have been conditioned to build upon, that self-gratifying self-government of pride and worse, greed. We are slowly taking away God's sovereignty by governing ourselves without His guidance. When this happens, before we know it, good becomes bad and bad good. Separations begin, then divisions, and if we do not put a stop to this in our own lives, when we die, the worst separation of all will happen; separation from God for eternity, hell.

    I was a family counselor for a couple of years, and when I would counsel husbands and wives, it was very evident that a common understanding between the couples kept emerging. They were trying to find happiness by living a 50/50 marriage. In the past I, too, was selfish in this area, and even worse. But now I know the scriptures do not teach this and my bosses and society didn't want me teaching anything from the Bible. I counseled anyway without saying so. I pointed out that a marriage that tried to live a 50/50 relationship only divides and eventually hurts the marriage because each spouse was trying to divide duties around the house, and score keeping in turn creates conflict. As scripture points out, by each man and wife living a 100/100 marriage, each begins to live for the other. Each begins to serve the other without keeping score because both are only focused on making the other happy, unconditional love. Once I got them to grasp that idea, both began to critique only themselves and start to better themselves for the benefit of the other.

This is the way God's true Church is.

I want to show you something else, statements that I want you to listen to. Then I want you to visualize and be honest how much you see any of these statements in your life;

- ➢ Indulgence instead of abstinence.
- ➢ Vital existents instead of spiritual pipe dreams.
- ➢ Undefiled wisdom instead of hypocritical self-deceit.
- ➢ Kindness to all instead of love wasted on ingrates.
- ➢ Vengeance instead of turning the other cheek.
- ➢ Responsibility to the responsible instead of concern for psychic vampires.

> Man as just another animal, sometimes better, more often worse than those that walk on all fours, who because of his "divine spiritual and intellectual development," has become the most vicious animal of all.
> All physical, mental, or emotional gratifications are a good experience.

Do any or all of these show themselves in you? Are any of these true in your life? If they are, please get on your knees and ask Jesus to give you strength to overcome them. You see, all of these statements are eight of the nine satanic statements of the satanic bible and show what satan stands for. The 9th one is;

> "Satan has been the best friend the Church has ever had, as he has kept it in business all these years."

Our society is changing in these ways before our eyes, and many are being deceived with its message. Please, hear what God is telling you and repent, then go and preach His word before so many more are lost. Self-satisfaction first, is just the beginning, or the cornerstone, of the great and abominable church. If you find it hard to let go of a weakness or sin because of your addiction to it, ask God for His help. If you put off disciplining yourself to read the Word of God and think that because you are kind or do not hurt anyone that you should be okay, then you are playing right into the devil's hands.

Today we see judges across our land making decisions that undermine the very foundation that gave birth to their authority. They find loopholes in the system to maximize their powers over the so-called balance of powers. We see a nation that once was proud to show its colors of red, white and blue representing "One Nation Under God," now we only whisper our support with like-minded people, being either ashamed or embarrassed to let anyone know we believe in a Christian God that inspired our forefathers to establish this great land.

Look at all aspects of your life. Love everyone yet do not their sins. Live by Jesus' example. Hate the sin, not the sinner. Love God with all your heart, mind, soul and strength, and love your neighbor as you would yourself, for there is no other commandment greater.

Let us finish with Psalm 105:1-5;

"O give thanks unto the Lord; call upon his name; make known his deed among the people. Sing unto him, sing

psalms unto him, talk ye of all his wondrous works. Glory ye in his holy name; let the heart of them rejoice that seek the Lord. Seek the Lord, and His strength; seek His face evermore. Remember His marvelous works that He hath done; His wonders, and the judgments of His mouth."

"And for the support of this Declaration, with a firm reliance on the protection of divine providence, we mutually pledge to each other our Lives, our Fortunes, and our sacred Honor."

> ~The ending covenant to God in our Declaration of Independence

Chapter Seven
Making a Covenant

Gaylord and Faye Shaw of Lamoni, Iowa, are close friends of our family and to me they are fine examples of Christians on earth who really live the Church. Gaylord has a PH.D. and is a professor of Biology, and Faye has her Masters in Teaching. Together they did a short study on covenants and made it into a nice presentation to share with others. I asked their permission to use it for this chapter because of how important making a covenant is in the walk we all seek with Christ. They said it would be okay but yet I want you to know that, again, I am not going to take everything they shared and write it down word for word; I want to share with you their study from my perspective as a modern day sinner, and my insight received from their study. I will, from the beginning of this chapter to the end, be putting down my understandings and comments.

The importance of a covenant is emphasized throughout the scriptures in the Old and New Testaments, and the Book of

Mormon. Each presents covenants the Lord has made with man. We see direct references to the new covenant in Luke 22:20; "likewise also the cup, after supper, saying, This cup is the new testament in my blood which is shed for you."

1 Corinthians 11:25; "After the same manner also he took the cup, when he had supped, saying This cup is the new testament in my blood; this do ye, as oft as ye drink it, in remembrance of me."

2 Corinthians 3:5-6; "Not that we are sufficient of ourselves to think any thing as of ourselves; but our sufficiency is of God; Who also hath made us able ministers of the new testament; not of the letter, but of the Spirit; for the letter killeth, but the Spirit giveth life."

Hebrews 8:8-10; "For finding fault with them, he saith, Behold, the days come, saith the Lord, when I will make a new covenant with the house of Israel and with the house of Jadah; Not according to the covenant that I made with their fathers, in the day when I took them by the hand to lead them out of the land of Egypt; because they continued not in my covenant, and I regarded them not, saith the Lord. For this is the covenant that I will make with the house of Israel after those days, saith the Lord; I will put my laws into their mind, and write them in their hearts; and I will be to them a God, and they shall be to me a people." Hebrews 9:15; "And for this cause he is the mediator of the new covenant, that by means of death, for the redemption of the transgressions that were under the first covenant, they which are called might receive the promise of eternal inheritance."

Notice two things about these passages, first, the word "testament" is synonymous with the word "covenant," and, second, these passages point out how just going through the motions, or physical aspects, of a covenant is not enough; but that we must begin to understand the spiritual aspects of a covenant. But like always, the adversary comes in and tries to deceive us into believing that man is smarter, or can be as smart as God, and beings to focus on our selfish desires over that of selfless service. This is why Jesus came down to give us the example and show us the way to everlasting glory. He did away with the old Covenant and began the New Covenant. Then again, over time a falling away began and a restoration of the New Covenant was needed. So God brought forward the record of another people whom He had led into the wilderness from Israel. Their record, the Book of Mormon, contained the fullness of Christ.

The book of Mormon is not named after the man Mormon, of whom there is record of within the book, but after a land where the people of Alma lived as Christ taught. And this was the place where the new covenant relationship was restored. **"And behold, I am called Mormon, being called after the Land of Mormon. The land in which Alma did establish the church among this people, yea, the first church which was established among them after their transgressions."** (3 Nephi 2:96)

We see the covenant mentioned in the title page of the Book of Mormon. " *Wherefore, it is an abridgement of the record of the people of Nephi, And also of the Lamanites.*

Written to the Lamanites which are a remnant of the house of Israel, And also to Jew and Gentile.

Written by way of commandment, And also by the spirit of prophecy and of revelation.

Written and sealed up and hid up unto the lord, that they might not be destroyed, To come forth by the gift and power of God, unto the interpretation thereof;

Sealed by the hand of Moroni and hid up unto the Lord, to come forth in due time by the way of Gentile, the interpretation thereof by the gift of God.

An abridgement taken from the book of Ether also, which is a record of the people of Jared, Which were scattered at the time of the Lord confounded the language of the people when they were building a tower to get to heaven--Which is to show unto the remnant of the house of Israel how great things the Lord hath done for their father, and that they may know the covenants of the Lord, that they are not cast off forever.

And also to the convincing of the Jew and Gentile that Jesus is the Christ, the Eternal God, manifesting Himself unto all nations.

And now if there be fault, it be the mistake of men; wherefore, condemn not the things of God, that ye may be found spotless at the judgment seat of Christ."

And again in Mormon 4:103,

"And may the Lord Jesus Christ grant that their prayers may be answered according to their faith; And may God the Father remember the covenant which He hath made with the house of Israel; And may He bless them forever, through faith on the name of Jesus Christ. Amen."

Yet again in Moroni 10:28;

"And awake! And arise from the dust, O Jerusalem! Yea, and put on thy beautiful garments, O daughter of Zion! And strengthen thy stakes and enlarge thy borders forever, that thou mayest no more be confounded, That the covenants of the Eternal God which He hath made unto thee, O house of Israel, may be fulfilled."

And to continue in Moroni 10:30,

"And again, if he by the grace of God are perfect in Christ and deny His power, Then are ye sanctified in Christ by the grace of God through the shedding of the blood of Christ, Which is in the covenant of the Father unto the remission of our sins, that ye become holy without spot."

For some of you reading this right now, this is the first time you have ever heard this. In Mark 4:9-10, we read; "**And when he was alone with the twelve and they that believed in him, they were about him with the twelve, asked of him the parable. And he said unto them, Unto you it is given to know the mystery** of the kingdom of God; but unto them that are without, all these things are done in parables." The lesson here is the closer we get to His word with study, fasting, and prayer, the more God will reveal to us. So do this that He might show you the truth in His mysteries.

1 Nephi 3:27-28 says; **"For He is the same yesterday, today, and forever; And the way is prepared for all men from the foundation of the world, if it so be that they repent and come unto Him."** Although God is always the same, when a covenant is broken or blessings are given to enhance man's ability to understand the fullness of the gospel, God changes the focus of His same law. When we look at the Old and New testaments in comparison, we see distinct changes in the focus. In the Old Covenant, the teachings were more focused on the law, punishment, justice, destruction, being cut off from God, forbidden fruit, misery, wickedness, bitterness, works, and death. With the New Covenant, the focus is more on the atonement, mercy, redemption, salvation, the presence of God, the tree of life, happiness, righteous, sweet grace, and life. **"And ye shall offer up unto Me no more shedding of blood, Yea, your sacrifices**

and your burnt offerings shall be done away, For I will accept none of your sacrifices and your burnt offerings; And ye shall offer for sacrifice unto Me a broken heart and a contrite spirit, him will I baptize with fire and with the Holy Ghost." (3 Nephi 4:49-50). This scripture shares the change of focus during the transition.

Covenants are very important in God's communications with us, and through out scripture God tells us of witnesses to His promises for us, witnesses such as a stone, Heaven and Earth, angels, the mood, a song, and baptism. Likewise, the adversary also has his covenants and witnesses. The world is a witness to the adversary of man's covenant to a temporal society. The difference here is our actions of selfishness is all that is needed to make a covenant with the devil. Within society there are examples of strong covenants following the way of evil, like the mafia, gangs, and secret clubs or organizations like the Free Masons, etc. But for the most part, the adversary's covenants go undetected as evil by being masked as self-gratificational experiences.

As we come to understand the importance of covenants,

and how they are very instrumental in our lives; we begin to see how much that someone's word, honesty, and promises play in our spiritual growth. All this in turn aides in the preparation of God's Kingdom.

God made one-sided covenants to Abraham that his descendents would become a people, receive a blessing, and have a land. God also made a promise to Noah in Genesis that "...neither shall there anymore be a flood to destroy the earth."

We also see conditional covenants like we find in Exodus 19:5-6; "Now therefore, if ye will obey my voice indeed, and keep my covenant, then ye shall be a peculiar treasure unto me above all people; for all the earth is mine; and ye shall be unto me a kingdom of priests and a holy nation. These are the words which thou shalt speak unto the children of Israel."

Over time covenants have been manipulated into petty and shallow gestures that people don't take seriously any longer, rather than being the strong tool of commitment they are suppose to demand. We read in the Doctrine and Covenants Section 83:8a, *"And your minds in times past have been darkened because of unbelief; and because you have treated lightly the* things you have received, which vanity and unbelief hath brought the whole church under condemnation." This is that tweaking over time that the devil does to us to deceive us. Then in the Doctrine and Covenants 83:8b, *"And this condemnation resteth upon the children of Zion, even all; and they shall remain under this condemnation until they repent and remember the new covenant, even the Book of Mormon and the former commandments which I have given them, not only to say, but to do according to that which I have written."*

We are still here today, and it is up to us to live the church. To come out of this condemnation we must understand the importance of our covenants. Let's start then by looking at what a covenant is. Some synonyms are; oath, vow, promise, contract, swear, "as the Lord liveth," and "As I live," among others. Some examples of current covenants are; marriage, business contracts, mortgages, and credit cards. Also, I spoke earlier, "my word is my bond," which is very rare today. Covenants are powerful when treated with the importance and respect they deserve. An example of the power of covenants is in Helaman 3:117-120;

"And now because thou hast done this with such unwaryingness, Behold, I will bless thee forever; and I will make thee mighty in word and in deed, in faith and in works; Yea, even that all things shall be done unto thee according to thy word, For thou shalt not ask that which is contrary to My will. Behold, thou are Nephi and I am God. Behold, I declare it unto thee in the presence of Mine angels, That ye shall have power over this people and shall smite the earth with famine and with pestilence and destruction, according to the wickedness of this people. Behold, I give unto you power that whatsoever ye shall seal on earth shall be sealed in heaven, and whatsoever ye shall loose on earth shall be loosed in heaven; And thus shall he have power among this people."

And also from Moroni 7:26, "And assuredly as Christ liveth, He spake these words unto our fathers, saying 'Whatsoever thing ye shall ask the Father in My name, which is good, in faith believing that ye shall receive, Behold, it shall be done unto you." The covenant relationship denotes the fullness of the gospel. We see this in Moroni's example in the book of Alma. "And Moroni was a strong and mighty man. he was a man of perfect understanding, Yea, a man that did not delight in bloodshed, a man whose soul did joy in the liberty and the freedom of his country and his brethren from bondage and slavery, Yea, a man whose heart did swell with thanksgiving to his God for the many privileges and blessings which he bestowed upon His people, A man who did labor exceedingly for the welfare and safety of his people, Yea, and he was a man who was firm in the faith of Christ—And he had sworn with an oath to defend his people, his rights, and his country and his religion, even to the loss of his blood." (21:132-134)

We all need to strive to achieve this fullness. This everlasting covenant that Genesis 9:22 I.V. explains; "And this is mine everlasting covenant, that when thy posterity shall embrace the truth, and look upward, then shall Zion look downward, and all the heavens shall shake with gladness, and the earth shall tremble with joy;"

Another good example of a covenant people is when we look at Alma at the waters of Mormon. We read in Mosiah 9:39-41, "And now as ye are desirous to come into the fold of God and to be called His people, and are willing to bear one another's burdens, that they may be light, Yea, and are willing to mourn with those that mourn, Yea, and comfort those that stand in need of comfort, and to stand as witnesses of God at all times and in all things and in all places that ye may be in, even until death, That ye may be redeemed of God and be numbered with those of the first resurrection, that ye may have eternal life–Now, I say unto you, if this be the desires of your hearts, What have you against being baptized in the name of the Lord as a witness before Him that ye have entered into a covenant with Him that ye will serve Him and keep His commandments, that He may pour out His Spirit more abundantly upon you?"

But in today's society how many of us actually take this covenant this seriously? Like the new modern Christian song says, "If we are the body, why aren't our arms reaching?..." There are many of us in the Christian community that need to come closer to God and His covenants so that we can go out and bring as many as we can to His kingdom. But first we must understand the importance of the covenant. Instead it seems we all want to fill our selfish desires with God's promises and are not willing to fulfill the desires He has for us. If we desire to be God-like as we say on Sundays and Wednesdays, then we must take seriously the covenant process. There is truth in promise. So when you do choose to take the step, that is when God's promise for you begins. That is His covenant to you. We see also in t he Doctrine and Covenants 17:7a-d a part of this covenant process, **"And again by way of commandment to the church concerning the manner of baptism: All those who humble themselves before God and desire to be baptized, and come forth with broken hearts and contrite spirits, and witness before the church that they have truly repented of all their sins, and are willing to take upon them the name of Jesus Christ, having a determination to serve him to the end, and truly manifest by their works that they have received of the Spirit of Christ unto the remission of their sins, shall be received by baptism into his church."**

God's Church not the denomination. This is always easier to say than to accomplish, especially in today's society with worldly influences that lack moral responsibility. But if we can weather through this, the Lord will bless us. In Helaman 3:115-116 we see that Nephi was blessed. **"Blessed art thou, Nephi, for those things which thou hast done; for I have beheld** how thou hast with unwearyingness declared the word which I have given unto thee unto this people; And thou hast not feared them and hast not sought thine own life, but hath sought My will and to keep My commandments."

Nephi was blessed according to God by his seeking God's will in all things no matter what. No matter what he wanted for himself. Selflessness for God's Kingdom.

Gaylord and Faye then asked a question in their presentation of covenants, "How do we get to a Golden Age?" Their answer was found in 3 Nephi 4:51-52, **"Behold, I have come unto the world to bring redemption unto the world--to save the from sins; Therefore, whoso repenteth and cometh unto Me as a little child, him will I receive, for of such is the Kingdom of God. Behold, for such I have laid down My life and have taken it up again; Therefore, repent and come unto Me, ye ends the earth, and be saved!"**

We see that through the resurrection of Jesus Christ was for the very purpose of mankind being able to be reborn. To truly repent of their sins and making a new covenant with God and for God and His kingdom. Again we see it in 3 Nephi

5:39-40 when Jesus says, "And again I say unto you, Ye must repent, and become as a little child, and be baptized in my name, or ye can in wise receive these things! And again I say unto you, Ye must repent, and be baptized in My name, and become as a little child, Or ye can in nowise inherit the kingdom of God."

When we do this, God gives us a little wisdom, and the more we focus on Him and His kingdom, the more insight is given unto us. In 2 Nephi 12:36-38 it says, "For behold, thus saith the Lord God: 'I will give unto the children of men, Line upon line of precept upon precept, Here a little and there a little; And blessed are they that hearken unto My precepts and lend an ear unto My counsel, For they shall learn wisdom; For unto him that receiveth, I will give more; And them that shall say, 'We have enough,' from them shall be taken away even that which they have."

If we as individuals do this, make and live out our covenants with God, then collectively the body of Christ will set the way for the kingdom of God. God will work in us and our covenants no matter where we are and bless the kingdom.

"And it came to pass that I, Nephi, beheld the power of

the Lamb of God, that it descended upon the saints of the church of the Lamb and upon the covenant people of the Lord which were scattered upon the face of the earth; And they were armed with righteousness and with the power of God in great glory." (1 Nephi 3:230-231)

In 2 Nephi 2:20-24 we read, "And that which shall be written by the fruit and thy loins, And also that which shall be written by the fruit of the loins of Judah, Shall grow together unto the confounding of false doctrines, and laying down of contentions, And establishing peace among the fruit of thy loins, and bringing them to the knowledge of their fathers in the latter days, and also to the knowledge of My covenants," saith the Lord; "and out of weakness he shall be made strong in that day when My work shall commence among all My people, unto the restoring thee, O house of Israel," saith the Lord."

This will happen, God's plan will make it happen to a covenant people; to a people willing to live the Church, live their covenant with God.

In Jeremiah 31:31-33 God says that a new covenant between the house of Israel and the house of Judah will happen and it did. "Behold, the days come, saith the Lord, that I will make a new covenant with the house of Israel, and with the house of Judah; Not according to the covenant that I made with their fathers in the day that I took them by the hand to bring them out of the land of Egypt; which my covenant they brake, although I was a husband unto them, saith the Lord; But this shall be the covenant that I will make with the house of Israel; After those days, saith the Lord, I will put my law in their inward parts, and write it in their hearts; and will be their God, and they shall be my people."

This new covenant is more than a p physical law to live by. It is a law of doctrine that is written upon our hearts. Then in verse 34 He gives another promise that He will remember their sins no more. So to get to the Golden Age, we must become a covenant people. Jesus tells us the kind of people we must be throughout 3 Nephi in the Book of Mormon, as well as through out the Gospels in the New Testament. In making covenants, the Hebrew have many symbolic reminders which they have used in the past, such as: Give the covenant terms, Exchange robes, Exchange belts, Cut the covenant, Raise right arms, Cut palms-mix blood, Make a scar, Exchange names, Eat a memorial meal, and Plant a memorial. These are all examples of symbolic reminders of the covenant. Whatever our symbolic gestures are, it is the living of the covenant that is the key to directing ourselves to the Golden Age. In Mosiah 3:6-8 we read;

"And we are willing to enter into a covenant with our God, to do His will and to be obedient to His commandments in all things that He shall command us all the remainder of our days, That we may not bring upon ourselves a never-ending torment as has been spoken by the angel, That we may not drink out of the cup of the wrath of God. And now, these are the words which King Benjamin desired of them and therefore he said unto them: 'Ye have spoken the words that I desired, And the covenant which ye have made is a righteous covenant. And now, because of the covenant which ye have made, ye shall be called the children of Christ, His sons and His daughters."

The kingdom of God becomes our purpose, and, through our living actively in our covenant to the Lord, we prepare the Kingdom for His coming. This is communing with Him. In a prayer Jesus gave concerning future believers, He said.

"Neither pray I for those alone, but for them also which shall believe on me through their word; That they all may be one; as thou, Father, are in me, and I in thee, that they also may be one in us; that the world may believe that thou hast sent me...I in them, and thou in me, that they may be made perfect in one; and that the world may know that thou hast sent me, and hast loved them, as thou hast loved me...And I have declared unto them thy name, and will declare it; that the love wherewith thou hast loved me may be in them, and I in them." (John 17:20-21, 23, 26)

Again, Moroni 10:29 shows us the garden tools to assist us in our quest. "Yea, come unto Christ and be perfected in Him and deny yourselves of all ungodliness, and if ye shall deny yourselves of all ungodliness and love God with all your might, mind, and strength, Then is His grace sufficient for you, that by His grace ye may be perfect in Christ; And if by the grace of God ye are perfect in Christ, ye can in no wise deny the power of God."

The final scripture used by the Shaws in their study follows:

"And again, if ye by the grace of God are perfect in Christ

and deny not His power, Then are ye sanctified in Christ by the grace of God through the shedding of the blood of Christ, Which is in the covenant of the Father unto the remission of your sins, that ye become holy without spot."

They emphasized the covenant of the Father is a grace that is given to us, because of the sacrificial steps Jesus took by shedding His blood for you and I. Now the ball is in our courts as individuals, so that collectively God will work through us to create the body of Christ, strengthen the body of Christ, which is the true Church of God.

"The Spirit of God working through man is like watching the burned coals of a camp fire work its glow from one ember to the next."

~Elder Jon Barney, 2001

Chapter Eight
The Gospel Purpose

Two days ago, June 22nd 2004, I finished chapter six, "The Kingdom of God vs. the Great Abominable Church," and I knew for chapter seven I was going to share with you a presentation/study by Gaylord and Faye Shaw, so I looked at my table of contents and wondered what the topic for chapter eight should be, but nothing specific came to mind. As I was asking God to show me, I knew that this week my denomination was having a week long reunion at Graceland University, in Lamoni Iowa. I looked at the schedule for the reunion that I had and saw a class the next morning that I should go to called the Gospel of the Kingdom, by Ronald K. Smith. The topic was close to the chapter I just finished, so I was drawn to it. So that morning I went to that class to find that it was the second day of a two-day class. Because of this, I just wanted to focus and see where the Lord wanted me to go from here.

Immediately I felt that this was good, and there was

something here the Lord wanted me to find for my needed topic. As the class ended I approached Mr. Smith and told him what I was working on and that I felt lead, not only here to this class, but to him. I couldn't put my finger on it, so I asked Mr. Smith to just take my diskette with the first six chapters on it and to read over it. As I took the workbook he made up for his class and said that I would take his work and study it, and then sometime soon we would get back together and discuss my first six chapters, and how they relate to the class he gave. He agreed, and we both went our separate ways.

That night I sat down, thinking that I would start his workbook trying to get some of it done. Before I started, I prayed and asked God to give me the strength and wisdom He wants for me, and if it be His will, to show me what it is He wants me to see. The whole workbook is only eleven pages long and it took scriptures from mainly the Inspired Version text but all could be found in the King James version as well. The first page took me through the book of Luke and asked questions concerning the Kingdom of God. His sixth question asked the reader, "When Jesus taught his disciples to pray, what was to be their first request?" It was during the Lord's prayer and, of course, the request was that "Thy Kingdom com." But because it was the Lord's prayer I kept reading it. When I got to the last sentence and read it, as I have done a thousand times before, the words just leaped out at me; "FOR THINE IS THE KINGDOM AND POWER, AMEN." If we look at the previous chapter in this book, we see that God is love. We learn that Jesus said that He is the kingdom, as well as the power. This began to have more meaning than ever before. I became excited, and the next thing I knew, I had finished the entire workbook. So much insight had come about the topic of this chapter that I was very eager to get started. This is not an effort to simply repeat what Mr. Smith had in his workbook, but to share the insight I received through the word of God given in this study relating to "The Gospel Purpose." It hit me like I was actually watching glorious pieces of God's puzzle of life come together. The next day I again met with Mr. Smith and gave him my testimony. In return he gave back my diskette, which he said he had not had a chance to read yet, But I told him I felt that I needed to start this chapter but I would be glad to discuss it with him when I was done. He agreed and seemed pleased at how I was responding to God's Spirit.

With that said, let's look at a summary of where we are so far in this book about the Gospel according to a modern day sinner.

In the first chapter I gave you a condensed version of my life's spiritual testimony to give you an idea of who I am and some of my experiences. I wanted to do this to show you that I was real with real life experiences, experiences some of you might be able to relate to as well. The second chapter started at the crucifixion because everything else in this book, as well as our lives, is set on this foundation of love He showed for you and I. The third chapter is probably the most complicated, but it is very essential in understanding how God physically interacts within us, and what His interaction can do for all His creation. The fourth chapter takes that understanding a little farther in living the Church and helps solidify chapter three's understanding. Chapter five then focuses on the understanding that we are now beginning to become aware of and shows us how obstacles can bog us down, and how we must negotiate these obstacles so we can reach the destination the Lord has for us. That brings us to chapter six which attempts to introduce the only two churches that exist on earth, God's and the devils. Chapter seven re-associates us with our personal relationship with God and the importance of not only understanding what a covenant is, but that we should individually make one with God so God can use that relationship along with those of others for His Kingdom.

Now we are in chapter eight. Here we will see the purpose of the Gospel, now that we understand its foundation.

Many years ago God created Adam and Eve. Scripture tells us they were the first humans created on earth. At no time in any scripture have I found that God commanded His people to create a club, organization, or committee, and then authorized them to rule over such with their own decisions, rules or traditions. Nowhere have I found a scripture that gives mankind a reason or hope to become ruler equal to, or above, God Himself. As a matter of fact, it seems to be just the contrary. All glory will be His. Our part is to be stewards, wardens if you will, governors of His law and of His sovereignty, and not rulers over what we ourselves create.

We have seen through history, since the time of Adam,

how God has given man gifts, so as to understand His love for us; and how man, through time or gradualism, grew to abandon God and His sovereignty, only then to be swept off the land of their inheritance. Time and time again we continue to make that mistake, the obstacle of "self." We must adhere to the Word of God, and, through our study, gain the knowledge that He will bring His kingdom by those who keep His commandments.

Now, my brothers and sisters let us look upon the Gospel Purpose. Why do I belong to the restoration denomination? I tell everyone that I can that I do not belong to the restoration denomination because I want to restore the Reorganized Church of Jesus Christ of The Latter Day Saints, because that would be to fall back into the same rut that caused that group to conform to the world and split for the second time. I belong to the restoration because I believe this remnant of people is in a prime position to restore the true Church of our living God through Jesus Christ. We need to understand that there are but two churches; understand that God is the same yesterday and today as He will be tomorrow, understand that the world has been stuck in a series of paradigms caused through the gradual process of man-governing denominations. This separates His people from him by traditions of man.

These traditions cause us to rest our salvation on the human leaders of a sect or denomination and to just go through the motions of a traditional worship, instead of individually making a covenant with God. These traditions only spawn misinterpretations, or a temporary state of safety in our own minds. This kind of attitude then helps with the separation of our spiritual life with that of our civil life as if they can actually be separated.

In our covenant with God we learn how important it is to actively keep a promise that in turn allows God to work through us. His love or presence is what we share with every creature around us. Since He is in and through all things, all things including us, because He is in them, have a relationship with Him. The relationship that God is having with those who understand is His kingdom, and His power. This is why all becomes His Glory.

I sat in a pew a couple weeks after I had preached a sermon on The Kingdom and listened to another brother preach against this kind of relationship. He said, "God is not a magical spirit that bounces from one to another." He agreed that God is a loving being but then continued that He is not some emotion that we feel. His intent was honorable because he was defending what he learned through the traditions of man. My covenant with God is one to not point my finger at my brother for his belief, but to speak on that which the Lord has put in my heart about my brother's condition of belief. Then, through prayer and fasting, I ask God to show me where I am wrong in my understanding, and when He shows me, to confess it. Then I continue to try and build His Kingdom. The Lord continues to let me know that He is mysterious and that there are many things we will not understand. God is "magical" to me if that means He says he can create the heavens and earth in six days and on the seventh, He rested. He is "magical" if that means His people can heal the blind, or make the cripple walk by simply placing their hands on them and allowing God to work His power through them. He is "magical" if that means He can send a host of heavenly angels to earth and give messages to His people and then disappear. You see, no matter how much education we receive from the world in sciences, psychology, etc. we will never be able to completely explain God. Nor will we ever be so educated that we become smarter than God. We might believe so through our egotistical mindset, but the truth is, we will never know unless God wants to reveal Himself to us.

This again brings us to the Gospel Purpose. Webster's Dictionary says that "gospel" is glad tidings; the revelation of the Christian faith; the story of Christ's life as found in the first four books of the New Testament; doctrine; belief accepted as infallibly true. This is good news and an infallible truth because the gospel is about Jesus Christ and what he accomplished by his resurrection. Webster tells us that "purpose" is an object in view; aim; end; plan; intention; effect. A purpose, then, is a view of something or things that we have to aim towards, an end that is an intentional plan to affect an outcome.

When we look at the Gospel Purpose what do we see? First, let's look at the purpose. The Gospel does in fact have an aim. That aim is directed solely at God's creation. Man is to be God's garden tools, or better put, tools that manage His creation with His power and His glory. How do we do this? By living the Church. By being members of His body. This is done by literally becoming aware of His presence in all things and understanding the guidelines set forth in His scriptures. His guidelines that we must understand is the good news that we seek in His word. The simple laws of the Ten Commandments that Moses shared with us are just the tip of many commandments that were a part of the old covenant. The golden rule, plus others, that Jesus not only shared with us but also demonstrated over His short thirty three years of human life is a part of the new covenant. Now we have the Book of Mormon which contains part of the old and new covenants brought to us by God's people and then later by Jesus Himself. All are gospels of God. The Zionic environment and the peace we seek are readily found in the Word of God. When we read, fast and pray we will come to an understanding of it. Achieving what we all seek begins with us, as individuals, living these understandings in every aspect of our lives, living the Church.

Once we grasp this concept, we in reality become members of His true Church. This is a part of the purpose, to become members of the True Church and to not be deceived by the devil's church and the paradigms we find ourselves in by manipulations of our adversary. Our man-governed egos are the devil's main focus. We are the bull's eye for his manipulations and his purposes.

Am I saying that we cannot belong to the True Church unless we try to live the Church as I described above? Yes, that is exactly what I am saying. The understanding of His law and His word is crucial to our eternal future or better put our future in eternity. We cannot simply belong to a man-made organization or denomination and expect to ride in on the coat tails of that group to our glorious destiny. You either belong to God's Church or the devil's. You cannot serve two masters.

Let's explain this a little further. The gospel is truth. The gospel is of Jesus the Christ. The key to understanding the gospel is through His resurrection. We are called through the gospel, 2 Thessalonians 2:14, We are begotten through the gospel, 1 Corinthians 4:15. God works in mysterious ways and this is no exception. *The resurrection of Jesus Christ shows us how His Church becomes His Kingdom.* This power of Gods' is actively working in all His creation as His Kingdom. Kingdom is defined by Webster as a "domain, one of the great divisions of natural history." We are the Church of the living God who is in and through all things. Jesus the head of the Church, Ephesians 5:28, lived as a human on earth to give us the example; so that after the resurrection we, as the body of the Church, Ephesians 4:12, can function in the holy triangle,(God, my neighbor and me), with an understanding of the gospel itself. His example and His resurrection shows us how He works in us and how He wants us to show others His Kingdom. It's magical I know.

Our purpose is to bring as many as we can unto the Kingdom of God by our examples of the body of Christ. *And so a purpose of the gospel is to show us the resurrection of Jesus Christ, so that we can edify the body of Christ.* Through this we come into the fold of the true Church. To edify is to instruct in moral religious convictions, to improve moral standings and by doing this we begin to prepare the way for His Kingdom here on earth. God moves through His Kingdom and when His Kingdom is in you because of your covenant with him, you have with you the power of God Himself. And we all know from 1 Corinthians 1:24 that Christ is the power of God and the wisdom of God.

Then in 1 Thessalonians 1:5 we read an explanation of this power.

In chapter three of Ephesians we read, "That he would grant you, according to the riches of His glory, to be strengthened with might by His Spirit in the inner man." The more we study the word of God, the more we realize His glory and the Kingdom that He himself abides in. It is among you and I right now, and that is our strength when we acknowledge him.

The book of John says; "Abide in me, and I in you. As the branch cannot bear fruit of itself, except it abide in the vine; no more can ye, except ye abide in me." (15:4) He continues to explain that we must live in God, and he in us in order for us to produce any fruit and without this, no fruit can be made. Then there is a wonderful promise in verse 7: "If ye abide in me, and my words abide in you, ye shall ask what ye will, and it shall be done unto you." Now you can see, this is how God is glorified; by our producing much fruit in His name, for His body, for His Church, for His Kingdom. Then Jesus tells the disciples again of loving your neighbor as I have loved you. He tells them that no man can have no greater love than to lay down your life for your friends. He did so for you and I.

As we grow in love and in this edifying of the body of Christ, His true Church, we grow in fellowship. Then when we feel that our burden is to great, we can lean on one another, and we will be there to help one another. If we falter in our covenant with Him, we have one another to help and pick us up from our fallen state. We all become friends and love ones in the body of Christ, the true Church, the Kingdom. We become guides, helpmates, a support group, after His example to prepare for His Kingdom. We can rest in Him and abide in Him. *This is the Gospel Purpose.*

Brothers and sisters, I know this is not easy. The Lord knows it as well. But you see, we must. We, as a people, we as believers in Him, must put aside our fears of ridicule, our condemning others, or our fear of the lack of popularity. God is counting on you as an individual to come unto Him, make your true covenant, and break away from the chains of man-made paradigms. Does that mean we can have a Church with no guidelines or rules? How will our services be run? Who is going to make decisions without our being man-governed? All these are good questions that I will try to touch on right now. To answer the first question of having a church with no guidelines or rules, this is not true. The body of Christ, or the Church has plenty of guidelines and rules to follow, in the scriptures, the word of God. Through our study, fasting, prayer and insight we must adhere to only the word of God. If the scriptures do not give us the guidelines that we seek, should we be seeking them? You see, all answers and guidelines are found in the word of God, and the things we find hard to get away from are the traditions that are set as man becomes complacent in our quest for that Zionic community, that Church, the Body of Christ. We get so caught up in the world around us that we begin to grow selfish instead of selfless. We begin to compare and critique other denominations and put our traditions above theirs. Our services are run by the Spirit of God. As far as the way we sit, lay down, or stand within the service really has no bearing or effect on the quality of the service. We can have just a wonderful service by sitting in pews all facing forward as we can by having everyone sit in a circle facing one another. Our priesthood can be put in charge of a service, yet it is through their preparations, fasting, and prayer prior to a service that inspires the body of Christ and as Christians, our participation in what ever Spirit led format the priesthood wants to use that day is what is going to edify the body of Christ. The preparation that individuals do prior to the service is collectively going to add to a service. A service is a learning environment as well as a sharing one. If the Spirit moves in a member of the body to share, then by all means it should be allowed so that all can receive what God is sharing with them. A service is, according to the guidelines in scripture and the methods of the gospel purpose, to edify the body of Christ. Chapter 9 in Hebrews explains the traditions of man were done away with by Christ giving Himself as the victim of our sins forever. We, as stewards of the Church, do not make decisions on our own authority, but by the authority of God which is found only in His Word through our study of the scriptures and our prayers and fasting for guidance from His Spirit.

Living the Church is becoming the Church. We must be willing to sacrifice our selfish worldly ways to accomplish this, and that is not an easy thing for us to do today while growing up in a selfish society. Step back from the paradigms we have been deceived into. See how this world is deceiving many to their destruction. Let go of your own selfish desires and work to get closer to God through study of His scriptures. Do this for your salvation, and find the calling God has for you to help bring others into the fold of the One True Church. *This is the Gospel Purpose.*

"The nature of God is a circle of which the centre is everywhere and the circumference is nowhere."

~ Anonymous

Chapter Nine
Some Final Thoughts

That is exactly what this short chapter is going to be, some final thoughts. I am going to write just what comes into my thoughts as I reflect on this book and its message.

First thought is that I would like for you to take the time and read these scriptures one right after the other. They have already been used in this book but this time without my interpretation of them. I ask you to be focused on yourself only and what the Spirit is telling you while you read His Word.

- Mark Chapter 12
- Colossians Chapter 3
- Psalms Chapter 1
- Ephesians Chapter 4
- Proverbs 3:1-4

Music has always been a pacifier to my spirit when worshiping and or pondering about my life and my relationship with God. I want to share a few with you here. The first one of course is **Amazing Grace**. I have heard this one many times in my life from a very young age but its message really didn't hit home until I came to realize how powerful His Grace really is. For many of us as modern day sinners we tend to overlook our blessings from His Grace in the first place, but once we really come to know Him we *can see* the path in which we had traveled and the tribulations we must continue to overcome by His Grace. I hope to have this played at my funeral by bag pipes some day.

The next one is **Holy, Holy, Holy**. And I really like it sang by a Christian Artist by the name of Phil Driscoe. His bluesy sound and trumpet really puts a lot of feeling into it. Again taken from God's Grace is His Mercy and in this song it seems to acknowledge God's strength and compassion that so many of us modern day sinners understand he must have to be able to forgive us of our many sins.

Just as I am I first heard as a little boy once when my mother was watching Rev. Billy Graham on television asking people to come to the front to accept Jesus as their savior. Now every time I hear this beautiful song and how it relates to those of us who know we have lived wicked lives, again, it shows the Grace

God has for us. No matter how bad you believe you are, no matter what you are wearing or the class in which you put yourself God loves you for who you are and wants you to come to Him and lay down all sins and accept His love for you, just as you are.

About every other year I go and visit my mother in Oklahoma and every time I do I can't help but to apologize to her for the awful child I was to her growing up. My mother had such a hard life and I remember times when she literally worked one full time job and three part time jobs to keep the financial ends meeting. I am so happy now that she has found her a good Christian man and she too has accepted Christ as her savior and she has never been happier. Anyway now every time I witness two things I remember my mother in prayer and those are marigolds and the song **The Old Old Path**. Her hard life and many struggles seem to be her doom until the Lord showed her the Old Old Path with all the compassion she yearned for.

Finally I can't go on without mentioning **The Battle Hymn of the Republic**. This song really is a song straight out of the foundation of this one nation under God. This song and it's patriotism for this blessed land are eroding along with the foundation. Our society as a whole does not take this truth forward any longer. The wedge between church and state is so embedded that our society (coyote) is slowly turning its back to God and the blessings he gave this land that we would be hard pressed to find those who will continue to march on with His truth.

I want to take a quick minute to tell of two books that I highly recommend that coincides with this book. First is a book written by a fellow ranger buddy Lt. Col. Dave Grossman called **Stop Teaching Our Kids to Kill**. Although it is not a religious book Colonial Grossman points out how we really are desensitizing our children to violence and death through television, movies, music, and video games. If you can get a hold of this book it will be worth your trouble.

The other book is **A Purpose Driven Life** by Rick Warren. I was given the tapes of this book when I had my rough draft of this book done. The tapes were given to me by my nephew Carlos who works with the Nascar circuit. This forty day study is exactly what a lot of people need today and both of these books become a great additional read to this book.

I guess there are other reflections I could share at this time but there are also many more studies I feel led to seek out for His Glory. Like the history of Moses, the Book of Job, America and how they might relate to this book and its message. So there might be time for this sharing at another time. But for now I ask you. Please practice and research the things you have read in this book, take them to God in prayer and in fasting and ask Him to show you the truth in His mysteries. Always remember, that His Kingdom, His Church, and His Message to you as an individual will be found with your agency, when choosing to walk the Old Old Path for His Glory. When you do this you will find your way from the depression, addictions, and many hardships that you face today. May our God Bless you all with a guiding light.

References:

- The Holy Bible, King James Version, 1992 Edititon
- The Holy Scriptures, Inspired Version, 1991 Edition
- The Book of Mormon, Restored Covenant Edition, 1999
- The Doctrine and Covenants, Enlarged and Improved Edition, 1955
- Webster's Pocket Dictionary, New International Edition, 2000

ISBN 1-41205839-2